P9-CEA-789

The Pecan Restaurant

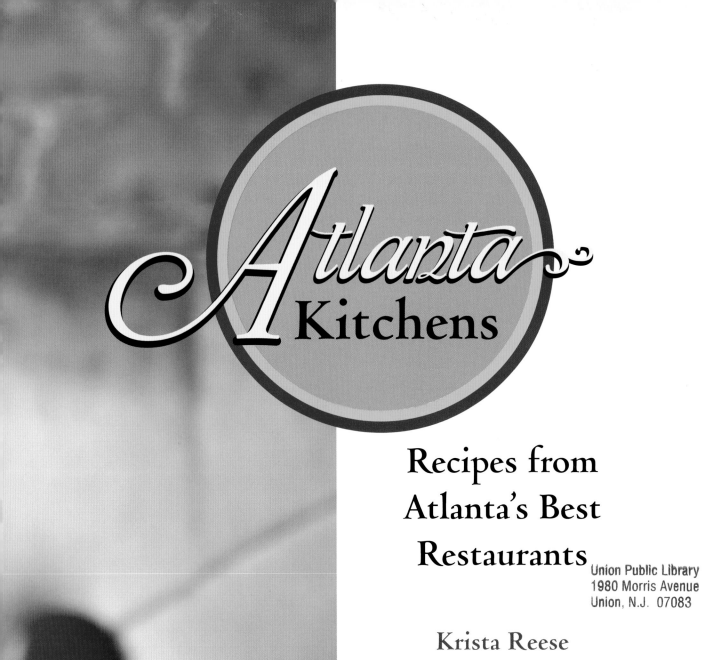

Atlanta Kitchens

Recipes from Atlanta's Best Restaurants

Krista Reese

Photographs by

Deborah Whitlaw Llewellyn

GIBBS SMITH

TO ENRICH AND INSPIRE HUMANKIND

Salt Lake City | Charleston | Santa Fe | Santa Barbara

First Edition
14 13 12 11 10   5 4 3 2 1

Text © 2010 Krista Reese
Photographs © 2010 Deborah Whitlaw Llewellyn

Published by
Gibbs Smith
P.O. Box 667
Layton, Utah 84041

1.800.835.4993 orders
www.gibbs-smith.com

Designed by Jocelyn Foye
Consulting by Janice Shay
Printed and bound in China
Gibbs Smith books are printed on either recycled, 100% post-consumer waste, FSC-certified papers or on paper produced from a 100% certified sustainable forest/controlled wood source.

Library of Congress Cataloging-in-Publication Data

Reese, Krista.
    Atlanta kitchens : recipes from Atlanta's best restaurants / Krista Reese ; photographs by Deborah Whitlaw Llewellyn. — 1st ed.
        p. cm.
    ISBN-13: 978-1-4236-0546-1
    ISBN-10: 1-4236-0546-2
    1. Cookery, American—Southern style. 2. Cookery—Georgia—Atlanta. 3. Cookery, International. 4. Restaurants—Georgia—Atlanta. I. Title.
    TX715.2.S68R45 2010
    641.5975—dc22
                                        2009030487

4th & Swift

Dedication

To everyone who ever fed me, in all the ways that count. Thanks.

Acknowledgments

My thanks to Susan Percy and Neely Young, my editors at Georgia Trend magazine, who keep sending me out in search of "bests." Thanks also to my husband, friends, and colleagues who supplied valuable suggestions and support, and to the Sunday Night Supper Club, who kept me in good food, drink, and company.

Contents

Rathbun Steak

Holy Taco

Introduction

I've always believed that cooks—like gardeners, knitters, and woodworkers—are among the best, most generous, and forgiving people on the planet. It has something to do with the happiness derived from making something with your own hands and sharing it with others in the form of cupcakes, zucchini, warm sweaters, end tables, and the like. That said, even allowing for cooks' naturally sunny dispositions, if you're looking through this book, it's probably because you love Atlanta and you've got certain opinions about what ought to be considered its best dishes. I'm hoping you'll flip through, nodding your assent at most of the choices, but inevitably (and perhaps immediately), you'll wonder, "Why on earth is this in here?" And: "Where in the world is . . . [fill in the blank with your favorite food]." Or even: "What kind of a pompous jerk could possibly proclaim herself judge of Atlanta's best dishes?"

I am this particular variety of pompous. For twenty years, I've enjoyed two distinct pleasures: living in Atlanta and writing about its restaurants—first at *Atlanta* magazine, as a contributor of short "Roundtable" reviews, then as dining editor; later as the *Atlanta Journal-Constitution*'s neighborhood "Restaurant Scout," and now as dining editor and critic at *Georgia Trend* magazine. It takes a certain chutzpah to be a critic, to expose your opinions to the public and invite disagreement. But that's nothing compared to the restaurateurs whose livelihoods depend on the long hours and backbreaking labor of running a restaurant and who expose their opinions to the public in the form of a menu. I've encountered my share of heated arguments. But my résumé makes me no more qualified to declare the best dishes in town than you are—that, of course, is subjective. It only gives me a chance to feature some of my favorites in print, with hopes that others will enjoy them as much as I do and that, in addition to finding some of their old favorites, they'll find some new ones too.

My experience has, however, lent me a front-row seat to our town's dynamic dining developments over the last two decades. Like most ink-stained wretches, when I first arrived here, I could barely afford to feed myself, so I jumped at the chance to try new restaurants on the company's dime. (Fortunately, all of my employers followed strict, old-school journalistic ethics: then as now, I was reimbursed for meals and expenses, and all visits were unannounced and undercover.) While I love the energy, enthusiasm, and style of many bloggers, I hope aspiring young food writers will find the same opportunities I did: to experience restaurants as any paying customer would, without the VIP fawning. That's how you find the real heart of a restaurant—if you're treated well when its owners think no one is looking.

Atmosphere, in fact, was one of my main criteria in choosing these restaurants. Now, in particular, we're all looking for more than good food at the right price. We want a communal life raft to cling to—preferably one with a party on board. New restaurants such as Dogwood, Holy Taco, Holeman & Finch, and Jay Swift's 4th & Swift join established brands like Goldberg's Deli, the Busy Bee Cafe, and Mary Mac's in addressing a particular community bound by their love of specialties like pork belly, a "grits bar," chopped chicken liver, ham hock, and pot likker. Their customers' joy at finding their heart's delight is almost palpable in these hotspots, and it's compounded by the setting and service.

I also chose restaurants that reflect the city's culinary range and depth. Woman cannot live by brioche alone, and even if I could, a constant diet from our most upscale fine dining establishments would surely lead to even crustier arteries than I currently possess. More importantly, I judge restaurants based on what they're trying to be, not what I wish they were. So I would never assess Barker's Hot

Dogs by the same standards as Kevin Rathbun's exciting, sophisticated dining rooms. Rathbun may have gone up against the Iron Chefs—and won—but I'm not sure he could pull off a scored and scorched red hot with the panache of a Barker's grill wrangler. And while several now-huge fast-food and chain restaurants have strong Atlanta roots or ties (Chik-fil-A, Krispy Kreme, the Waffle House), I opted to go with independents and mom-and-pop establishments. (Exceptions: Hotel restaurants that are both unique and Atlanta "bests.") I also excluded the big names you now find in many big dining towns: Tom Colicchio and Jean-Georges Vongerichten are nationally and internationally famous and operate the high-profile, well-respected Craft and Spice Market restaurants, but they're not Atlanta chefs.

Next, I wanted to highlight local ingredients that serve as a kind of literal oral tradition: Georgia's heirloom tomatoes, Silver Queen corn, Vidalia onions, and, of course, peaches feed the whole country, but perhaps no one enjoys them more, and in as many ways, than we do. Add mountain-stream trout, Tybee Island shrimp, and quail from the red-clay plains, and you've got a picture of our state's landscape and agriculture: uniquely Southern, but also incredibly diverse, with almost every kind of ecosystem from beach to mountain to desert, not to mention the plush green Piedmont that shades Atlanta's leafy neighborhoods. We Georgians are lucky—we have the world in a state. And increasingly, Atlanta restaurants are recognizing the value of having this varied bounty so close at hand.

Beyond that nearly indefinable feeling of belonging in a great restaurant and our state's

Kevin Rathbun at Rathbun's.

signature ingredients, I also wanted to include the dishes that leap to mind specifically when you think of Atlanta. Which are . . . um . . . well, what? Unlike other Southern cities like Savannah, Charleston, and New Orleans, Atlanta, it seems, is too young and restless to have historic, iconic dishes—we really have no equivalent to their Country Captains, syllabubs, and gumbos. With the exception of one local elixir—Coca-Cola, which the High Museum's Table 1280 enshrines in an entirely appropriate cocktail (see page 219)—few ingredients or dishes immediately conjure the busy town local rappers affectionately refer to by airport code: the ATL. Instead, most Atlantans will cite their culinary heritage as old-school, generic Southern favorites: smothered pork chops; green beans pressure-cooked to near-pudding; lacy-edged cornbread; fried okra; barbecue; iced tea with hair-perming sweetness; and perhaps most of all, fried chicken—so typically Atlanta I've included several versions. Each restaurant's approach, from Son's Place to the Ritz Café, is dramatically different yet bona-fide Southern fried.

These foods were often the creative triumphs of Southern cooks who had little to work with besides some scrawny yard birds, stone-ground cornmeal, and their own subsistence farms. (Today, of course, those free-range, whole-grain, and organic ingredients would trigger a stampede at any gourmet fresh market.) But from its destitute post–Civil War days, Atlanta has slowly grown into one of the nation's biggest port cities (an airport, but a port nonetheless). Like our symbol, the phoenix, the city rose from smoldering ashes and reinvented itself. That transformation has accompanied a fascinating evolution of what it means to be an Atlantan. Once provincial and prosaic, Atlanta is now a multi-dimensional melting pot, with new residents re-creating the foods they enjoyed in exotic homelands like Eritrea, Somalia, or even south Texas. As a result, our dining scene simmers with activity, with scores of ethnic, international, regional, and just plain exciting restaurants bubbling up from the stew.

As late as 1988, when I moved here from New York, good Chinese and Mexican restaurants were hard to find. I was overjoyed to rediscover the dishes of my Southern family and schooling. Oh how I'd missed good iced tea, buttery grits, and real country ham!

Grand China Duck with Beautiful Leeks, page 106

But soon I longed for the clanging, steamy delights of Chinatown and Little Italy's bakeries, and the tiny Burmese restaurant next door to me in SoHo. I dreamed of the Upper West Side's Ethiopian and Salvadorian restaurants and fell into reveries about the local specialties I'd found on trips to Hong Kong, Paris, London, and the small silver mining towns and coastal resorts of Mexico.

In Atlanta, I could continue my travels on Buford Highway, where Vietnamese and Korean spots crowded Asian groceries and Chinese noodle shops, as well as Hispanic pool halls and taco drive-throughs. Today, Buford Highway's thriving commercial district stretches for miles, and this immigrant's street of dreams offers innumerable foodie finds, from banh mi sandwiches and Korean barbecue to Peruvian, Ethiopian, and Bangladeshi specialties. In Clarkston and

Park 75 Restaurant

Scottdale, you can try Eritrean dishes and Halal pizza. In Marietta, you'll find Brazilian bakeries and cleverly Americanized Indian fast food spots.

More importantly, a few cuisines once considered exotic are no longer limited to immigrant byways—they've joined the ranks of Atlanta's most stylish and upscale restaurants with critical raves to match their lavish environments along Buckhead's priciest Peachtree Road real estate. Brothers Chris and Alex Kinjo bring their shared Vietnamese-Japanese heritage to the fore in their beautiful, inventive restaurants, including Nam, MF Sushibar, and the stunning MF Buckhead. Midtown's late, lamented Cuerno celebrated Spain's exciting culinary offerings, from tapas to authentic paellas (not to mention the charging deconstructed bull sculpture in the dining room). Longtime restaurateur Pano Karatassos' tribute to his homeland, Kyma, is perhaps the most upscale Greek restaurant in the country. And in Repast, the only fusion restaurant I've ever truly loved, husband-and-wife chefs Joe Truex and Mihoku Obunai manage to gracefully reconcile their native cuisines of Louisiana and Japan—sometimes in the same dish.

If you are not a cook, I hope you will enjoy this cookbook as a restaurant guide or perhaps simply as a sort of time capsule of what it's like to live in Atlanta right now. Restaurants are at least as valid a map of history as census charts and demographic maps. One day our dining habits will seem as quaint as our forebears' fondness for mock turtle soup, tied to cultural and economic forces that we're too close to see right now. But hindsight is not only more acute, it also provides the big picture.

At the Atlanta History Center, you can slip on white gloves to turn the fragile pages of the *Atlanta Journal Sunday Magazine*. There, stories of Atlanta's early twentieth-century social life spring to life with vivid photographs above bylines that include Margaret "Peggy" Mitchell and food editor Mrs. S. R. Dull. Mitchell's mischievous, elfin face and figure are the opposite of Mrs. Dull's stern and formidable visage, but like Mitchell's *Gone With the Wind*, the beloved food writer's best-known work, the 1928 cookbook *Southern Cooking* is still in print.

It took a while for Atlantans to embrace restaurants. Beyond short-order grills and lunch counters, dinner parties were much more socially acceptable, though some dined in private clubs like the one at the Kimball House, the city's first luxury hotel, built just after the Civil War. But by the 1940s, as the South climbed from poverty, restaurants slowly began to emerge, most of them modest home-style establishments like Mary Mac's Tea Room, in business since 1945. Achieving that kind of longevity in a city that has torn down so many of its most beloved landmarks is nothing short of remarkable.

Look at any era of Atlanta restaurants and you'll get a taste of life here at the time. Surprisingly, even in its earliest restaurant days, Atlanta always featured international cuisine—a 1946 Atlanta Yellow Pages lists Chinese, French, and Italian restaurants (featuring "Italian spaghetti with Roman cheese"). The fascinating then-and-now collection of photos at the Atlanta Time Machine website (www.atlantatimemachine.com) chronicles our town's two-decade-long fascination with tiki culture at places like Trader Eng's, Bamboo, Mai Tai, the Malibu, the Dobbs House Tiki, the Paradise Room at the Henry Grady Hotel, and the Polynesian Lounge at the Atlanta Biltmore Hotel ("overlooking the Biltmore pool. . . . Exotic beverages and delicacies served in an atmosphere of tropical enchantment").

It's an Atlanta I never had a chance to see, but which still lives in the minds of the people who frequented those spots—and others long gone. Those places (and the illustrations of the palm trees, umbrellas, and tiki huts that accompany them) are a tantalizing glimpse of Atlanta in the 1950s through '70s. You can almost imagine the men in their skinny ties and sharkskin suits escorting women in murmuring taffeta cocktail dresses through dining rooms lit by dancers' flaming torches.

Some restaurants need only be named to conjure an entire era: The Frances Virginia Tea Room, opened in 1928, lured well-heeled matrons with its dainty sandwiches and convenient location near high-end downtown stores like Regenstein's for more than thirty-five years. Herren's drew businessmen and families with its famous sweet rolls and the city's first lobster tanks. The Coach & Six emanated an exclusive Buckhead aura from its glowing, gas-lit courtyard. Harrison's was home to a rowdy, sports-loving crowd including Lewis Grizzard and the "Buckhead Boys." The fledgling Buckhead Rotary Club bought their lunches at Hart's for $1.25 in 1950. Manuel's Tavern, a once-smoky bar established in 1956, still serves wings and

Buckhead Diner

Ecco

burgers to an eclectic assortment of writers, cops, pols, bikers, and baseball fans.

Restaurants also rode—and crashed—on political waves. Franklin Garrett's Atlanta and Environs states that in 1942, only fourteen foreign-born Japanese lived in Atlanta, one of them Sadajiro Yoshinuma, known to "thousands of Atlantans who patronized the restaurant and nightclub Wisteria Garden on Peachtree Street." By December 27, a little over a year after Pearl Harbor and the ensuing declaration of war on Japan, the Atlanta Constitution lists a notice for a court-ordered auction of the restaurant's assets, which "until recently enjoyed exceptionally good patronage."

Atlanta restaurateurs played a far more important role than just feeding customers in the 1950s and '60s, as their enterprises became social battlegrounds. The city's public life was revolutionized, quietly and not so quietly, in upscale cafes like The Magnolia Tea Room at Rich's and countless downtown lunch counters. There, young Atlantans like Martin Luther King Jr. and Julian Bond, with black and white ministers and students from local colleges, endured the taunts, insults, and physical assaults of enraged whites who believed blacks had no right to sit among them for a cup of coffee.

One Atlanta restaurant skirmish may have actually influenced the outcome of a presidential election. For his protest at the Magnolia Tea Room, MLK Jr. was arrested and jailed, and then moved during the night to the notorious Reidsville Prison. His terrified family and friends publicly pleaded for help, prompting reporters to ask the 1960 presidential candidates for their reactions to

MLK Jr.'s imprisonment. After candidate John F. Kennedy's brother Robert personally appealed to the judge overseeing the case, King was freed. The move won Kennedy broad African-American support. Richard Nixon, Kennedy's opponent, declined to comment or act on King's arrest and lost an extremely tight election that saw record African-American voting.

The protests continued, even as the rest of the country looked on in horror and Atlanta's reputation as "The City Too Busy to Hate" frayed: proprietors often dragged integrationists—who'd pledged nonviolent non-cooperation—from their establishments. Though they often demanded protestors' arrests, few restaurateurs risked pressing charges—the Supreme Court had already overturned such convictions on grounds of discrimination.

Behind the scenes, forward-thinking civic leaders like Mayor William Hartsfield and his successor, Ivan Allen Jr., quietly worked with the protestors to integrate Atlanta peacefully . . . if slowly. With Hartsfield, Allen, and Gov. Ernest Vandiver appealing to their reluctant segregationist constituents, King, Lonnie Smith, and Bond managed to coalesce older, more conservative community leaders with their activist peers. The University of Georgia began integrating the state's public schools in 1961, but there were still holdouts among private commercial establishments. Most notorious was Lester Maddox, who stood at the door of his downtown cafeteria, The Pickrick, wielding an ax handle to deny blacks' entrance despite passage of the 1964 Civil Rights Act. (Maddox would close his fried-chicken emporium in 1965 rather than comply.)

Atlanta still had a long road to travel. Maddox, in an election fluke, would later sit in the Governor's Mansion, and in his later years would protest his enduring reputation as a racist, pointing to his progressive accomplishments in office. Nevertheless, long before Maddox's show of force, and with considerable risk, other more enlightened souls quietly integrated their restaurants before it became law. Perhaps the first was Ma Sutton's, a legendary boardinghouse/tea room on Auburn Avenue (the "black Wall Street" before it became Sweet Auburn). Most of her patrons were black and couldn't enter white establishments, but if a white serviceman

Mary Mac's Fried Chicken, page 96

came home during World War II and wanted to eat with his buddy, the two would be served there without a problem. It would take twenty years, but a few white establishments would eventually join them, preceding legal mandates—Herren's, quietly, in the early '60s, and Mary Mac's under second owner Margaret Lupo, around the same time.

Like Frances Virginia Wikle Whitaker before her, Mary Mac's founder, Mary McKinsey, faced her own challenges. Both knew better than to call their establishments a restaurant—in the South, that would have been unacceptably unladylike. As late as the 1940s in Atlanta, unescorted women were routinely arrested for suspicion of prostitution if they were discovered engaged in such shocking acts as lingering over a burger in a restaurant—it certainly wouldn't do to be known for operating one. Despite the hearty menu suitable for field hands, Mary Mac's was (and is) a "Tea Room." In the '40s, it was one of many operated by war widows desperate to earn a living.

Scott Peacock at Watershed

Another ingenious businesswoman, Mary Jordan, arrived in Atlanta in the '20s. The daughter of sharecroppers, Jordan was confident enough in her cooking to go door-to-door in wealthy Buckhead seeking catering work. She made her own break when a desperate matron hired her at the last minute for a party, despite having little in her pantry but some wizened old turnips. Jordan's centerpiece—a turnip mold with cheese sauce—was such a hit she rarely lacked work from then on. Adept at traversing Atlanta's increasingly blurry color lines, Jordan became the go-to caterer for many elite business, legal, and political gatherings. Her son, Vernon Jordan, later a civil rights hero, presidential advisor, and Washington powerhouse attorney, would write that he learned his considerable oratory skills by listening to speakers as he worked at his mother's jobs. Mary Jordan became one of Atlanta's best-known African-American millionaires and philanthropists. The Jordan family continued operating her catering company long after her death.

Many restaurants, however, abruptly disappeared through the years—and to some, good riddance. (One acquaintance who remembers the Pickrick's fried chicken gives this one-word assessment: "Soggy.") Gone too are haunts where MLK Jr. and his lieutenants, like future Mayor Andrew Young and Ralph David Abernathy, strategized over barbecue (Aleck's Barbecue Heaven) and listened to jazz. La Carrousel, a nightclub at the original Paschal's on MLK Drive, where Aretha Franklin, Lena Horne, and Dizzy Gillespie entertained, was torn down and never replaced when Paschal's relocated to a more upscale spot on Northside Drive. Strategic headquarters for civil rights leaders, Paschal's served black and white patrons in the '50s, and they danced together at La Carrousel.

In February 2009, events came full circle with a proposal that would bind these two famous fried chicken restaurants representing the South's past and its future, and only a short distance apart. Rep. John Lewis, one of King's closest associates, survived many violent attacks (including a life-threatening head injury during the March on Selma) to become Atlanta's long-term Fifth District Congressman. Lewis suggested that the old Pickrick site, currently part of the Georgia Tech campus and slated for demolition, should be preserved. It could be linked, Lewis proposed, by a "civil rights trail" to another building now scheduled for destruction by its landlord, Clark Atlanta University—the original Paschal's.

Atlanta's comparatively peaceful struggles—and integrationists' eventual victory—saved it from irrelevance. As a new generation, including Maynard Jackson and Andrew Young, stepped into civic leadership roles, the city grew into a business powerhouse, operating the nation's busiest airport and attracting an enviable collection of national and international company headquarters. That, of course, was very good news for its restaurants. More milestones passed: Nathalie Dupree's 1970s cooking school at Rich's graduated distinguished chefs like cookbook author Shirley Corriher. Pano Karatassos opened Pano's & Paul's, one of the city's first serious fine-dining restaurants that was also a popular smash. Chef Guenter Seeger drew the city's first Mobil five-star ranking at the Buckhead Ritz-Carlton's Dining Room.

Today, Atlanta is a dynamic restaurant town, still evolving—perhaps even more rapidly than most because of the current economic climate. We're among the most wired cities in the nation, with one of the longest commutes, meaning that when we finally get home, we're more likely to look for our favorite dishes in restaurants than in the fridge. Once there, we often spend more per capita on meals. As satellite communities sprout, with walkable neighborhoods and several destination restaurant neighborhoods (East Atlanta Village, Midtown, Buckhead, Virginia-Highland, Old Fourth Ward, Castleberry), Atlanta is forging its dining identity, brick by brick.

No longer is our town content to mimic others' big-city scenes as if they'd set the template for regional success and our own had little worth. To the other ghostly restaurant names of past eras, add another: Seeger's, the thrillingly contemporary and cutting-edge restaurant from the German chef who left the Ritz to open his own place. His techniques—using classic European methods with local, organic ingredients—brought a national spotlight to Atlanta. Alas, his day ended in 2006, but Seeger's helped validate the value of our own bounty, as well as training a next generation of chefs for their own kitchens. Chef Shaun Doty of Shaun's is just one of his former acolytes.

Seeger's closing was also a turning point for Atlantans to begin to appreciate their own cuisine. For too long, Americans valued their own chefs' abilities to imitate European methods. Julia Child may have introduced an appreciation for good food and classic techniques, but food snobs also translated into it a disdain for native dishes. When Alice Waters, on the West Coast, trumpeted the arrival of a new and uniquely American cuisine based on local, seasonal ingredients, it was only a matter of time until the rest of the country rediscovered its own regional culinary contributions.

Finally, Atlanta chefs are among them, with serious creative talents like Scott Peacock, Linton Hopkins, Jay Swift, and the Ritz Café's Bennett Hollberg treating our peaches, grits, and fried chicken with the respect they deserve. Peacock and his mentor, the late Edna Lewis, in particular, broke ground in acknowledging and joining the accomplishments of the black and white chefs who invented Southern cuisine. Critics are taking note. No longer are they like the early Colonial intellectuals who kept listening for the first strains of a new and truly American classical music—if only they could hear it over those damned banjos!

Just as those tiki restaurants represent a grainy Polaroid snapshot of Atlanta in the early 1960s, this book is a little hologram of our city right now. Inside, you'll find some of the town's popular and foodie favorites, including some long-running classics and a few glimpses of the future. Here, too, is Atlanta's melting pot, with Ethiopian, Thai, Chinese, Vietnamese, and Indian offerings. Dip in your spoon for a taste.

Linton Hopkins at
Restaurant Eugene

As we go to press, a few restaurants that agreed to participate in this book have closed their doors. The downturn's casualties seem to represent nearly every restaurant strata: The Globe was an ambitious, hip hangout in midtown's Technology Corridor. The young people who were its customers were likely among the first victims as the economy stalled. Another, Son's Place, was soul food heir of fried chicken king Deacon Burton. And as summer turned to fall, Atlanta was stunned to learn the critically acclaimed Ritz-Carlton Buckhead Dining Room would soon turn dark.

However, some restaurants also found themselves evolving: Pano's & Paul's, is ending its long, halcyon run but also evolving into its own heir—Pano's, to be located in one of Atlanta's new posh hotels, the St. Regis. Restaurateur Pano Karatassos, whose first restaurant spawned a whole group of high-end, highly respected eateries, knows that when one door closes, another opens. Like all those once-thriving establishments, these recently stilled dining rooms are now fixed in amber, memories of an Atlanta on the way to its future.

—Krista Reese

Cobb Salad and Sun Tea
Sundial

Appetizers
Good to Go

From its beginnings, Atlanta has always been a crossroads. Once Terminus, then Marthasville, it was a place between North and South, "back East" and the frontier, the mountains and the sea. People met and stayed, sometimes for a few years, a season, or maybe just long enough for a meal before catching the train and moving on. That's right—our city has long been a kind of overgrown version of the Hartsfield Airport waiting room. Fortunately, the food is much better.

Our city's transient nature often translates into a lack of respect for our history but also injects an ambitious, forward-moving energy. It all comes together in the heart of the city, where our freeways join like huge human arteries and separate again to distribute commuters in all directions, toward home. If you're an Atlantan, you know what it's like to sit in traffic—and to plan your life around it. That means we are often grabbing bites here and there before moving on to the next plate. If we're at the end of our day, we can breathe a sigh of relief and stretch the evening meal to a leisurely three courses, beginning with a civilized introduction perhaps made to accompany a cocktail. That first course is a jump-start after a dull day, something so savory and piquant that it opens you up to a whole new consideration of everything that will follow. Sometimes these dishes are enough to stretch into a full meal once you add bread and a salad. But more often than not, these little gems are just enough to get us to our next destination.

Pimento Cheese

WATERSHED, CHEF SCOTT PEACOCK

Serves 6

There are as many versions of "minner cheese" as there are cooks, and Scott Peacock's takes the old-fashioned route, with homemade mayonnaise and roasted peppers.

2½ cups grated extra-sharp cheddar cheese, at room temperature

¾ cup homemade mayonnaise

3 tablespoons finely chopped, peeled, and seeded
    roasted red bell pepper or pimento

⅛ teaspoon cayenne pepper, or to taste

5 to 6 grinds black pepper

Salt (optional)

Celery sticks, to serve

Combine the cheese, mayonnaise, bell pepper, cayenne, and black pepper in a mixing bowl and stir until well mixed and creamy. Taste carefully for seasoning and adjust as needed. Cover and store, refrigerated, until ready to serve.

Soak the celery sticks in ice water for 30 minutes. Remove the pimento cheese from the refrigerator 15–20 minutes before serving.

Drain the celery sticks and serve with the pimento cheese.

Homemade Potato Chips with Warm Maytag Blue Cheese

BUCKHEAD DINER, BUCKHEAD
LIFE RESTAURANT GROUP

Serves 12

With its gleaming chrome exterior and handsome dark wood paneling inside, the Buckhead Diner draws a dedicated crowd of businesspeople to its high-profile Piedmont Road location—many of them for this, the restaurant's best-known dish.

Potato Chips

50 Idaho potatoes

Salt to taste

Blue Cheese Sauce

3$\frac{1}{8}$ cups whole milk

$\frac{1}{4}$ cup butter

3$\frac{1}{2}$ cups heavy cream

1 pound cream cheese

1 pound plus 4 cups blue cheese crumbles

8 ounces Parmesan cheese, freshly grated

Peel the potatoes and place in a bucket of cold water for a few minutes to chill. Remove and slice into thin rounds. Do not salt. Cook at 320 degrees F in a fryer or large skillet until light golden in color. Drain on paper towels and salt to taste.

Preheat the oven to 350 degrees F.

Combine the milk, butter, heavy cream, and cream cheese in a heavy-bottomed saucepan over low heat and cook until just beginning to simmer, stirring frequently. Watch carefully; the sauce is easily scalded. Remove from the heat. Stir in the pound of blue cheese and the Parmesan cheese. Puree with a hand blender until smooth.

Spoon a little of the sauce onto the bottom of an ovenproof plate. Add a layer of chips, drizzle with sauce, sprinkle with 2 cups blue cheese and repeat to make two layers. Heat in the oven for 3 minutes at 350 degrees F until the blue cheese on top start to melt.

Salt and Pepper Squid

HONG KONG HARBOUR, OWNER PING LIM

Serves 6

One of the first in-town Chinese restaurants to serve dim sum in the mornings and everything else late at night, Hong Kong Harbour also serves up fresh crab and lobsters from its bubbling tanks.

1 pound calamari (squid) bodies, cleaned
¼ cup Szechuan peppercorns
¼ cup sea salt, finely ground
2 cups flour
2 cups cornstarch
1½ cups peanut oil

Slice the calamari bodies down one side and open them up to lie flat. Cut the calamari on the inside to open them up. Set aside.

Heat a small dry skillet over high heat. Add the peppercorns and toast for a few minutes, stirring constantly, until they start to sizzle and pop. Remove them from the pan and set aside. Add the salt to the pan and cook over high heat until it has turned a gray color. Remove from heat. Grind the salt and peppercorns with a spice grinder to a fine powder. Transfer to a resealable plastic bag and mix in the flour and cornstarch.

Heat the oil in a wok or heavy skillet over high heat until very hot. Place a few pieces of calamari at a time into the bag and shake to coat. Shake off the excess and quickly fry them in the oil until browned, turning once. Each one should take about 30 seconds. Serve immediately.

Strawberry Serrano Mussels

BABETTE'S CAFÉ, CHEF/OWNER MARLA ADAMS

Serves 6

Strawberry Serrano Base

3 cups strawberries, hulled

3 serrano peppers, seeded

¾ teaspoon minced garlic

¾ teaspoon minced shallot

2 teaspoons cream of coconut (Coco Lopez brand is recommended)

Mussels

6 pounds mussels, cleaned

1½ cups heavy cream

¾ cup unsalted butter, at room temperature

¾ cup white wine

Salt and freshly ground black pepper, to taste

Juice of ½ lemon, or to taste

2 tablespoons chives cut in 2-inch lengths, for garnish

To make the strawberry base, combine the strawberries, peppers, garlic, shallot, and cream of coconut in a food processor and puree until completely smooth.

Pour 1½ cups of the strawberry mixture into a large saucepan. Add the mussels, cream, butter, wine, and salt and pepper. Cover with a lid, set over high heat, and cook until the shells open. (Discard any that do not open.) Add the lemon juice, toss, and add more salt and pepper if needed.

To serve, turn out into a bowl and garnish with chives.

Key West Rock Shrimp Pirozhki with Béarnaise Sauce

NIKOLAI'S ROOF, CHEF OLIVIER DE BRUSSCHERE

Serves 6

Atlanta's longtime favorite special occasion (and expense account) restaurant atop the Atlanta Hilton has an unusual concept: food that might have been served to the Russian aristocracy (thus the name, for Nikolai Romanov). Much of the menu is classic French, but the nods to Russian food include plenty of caviar, vodka, and the little stuffed dumpling known as pirozhki.

Pirozhki

- 3 tablespoons unsalted butter
- 4 shallots, chopped
- 3 cloves garlic, chopped
- 2½ pounds ground cooked Key West rock shrimp, peeled (regular shrimp can be substituted but lobster tail is a better substitute, as it is sweeter)
- 1 splash brandy
- 1 tablespoon tomato paste
- 1½ cups shrimp stock
- 4 tablespoons fresh tarragon, chopped
- 4 basil leaves, finely chopped
- Salt and freshly ground black pepper
- ½ cup heavy cream
- 2 ounces fresh bread crumbs
- 2 (9½ x 9¼-inch) sheets puff pastry, defrosted if frozen
- 2 large eggs
- 2 tablespoons cold water
- Flour, for dusting

Béarnaise Sauce

- 2 large egg yolks
- 2 tablespoons white wine
- 1 tablespoon lemon juice
- 1 tablespoon cold water
- 2 cups clarified butter
- 1 tablespoon chopped fresh tarragon
- Salt and freshly ground black pepper

To make the pirozhki, melt the butter over medium-high heat. Add the shallots and garlic and sauté until fragrant, about 30 seconds.

Add the shrimp and continue to sauté for about 4 minutes, stirring. Add the brandy and boil to remove the alcohol. Stir in the tomato paste until well blended. Pour in the shrimp stock, bring to a boil, and cook until the liquid is almost completely boiled off, stirring frequently. Add the tarragon and basil and season to taste with salt and pepper. Add the heavy cream, bring to a boil, and allow to cook for about 5 minutes. Remove from the heat and mix in the bread crumbs. Place in the refrigerator until cooled.

Preheat the oven to 350 degrees F.

Use an 18-8 ice cream scoop to portion out three balls of the shrimp mixture per person. If your scoop is a different size, adjust the presentation accordingly. The balls should fit on the pastry 1 inch apart, 3 per serving. Mix the eggs with the water until a smooth emulsion has formed.

Lightly brush the pastry with the egg mixture and line up the balls on the sheet, leaving approximately 1 inch of space between them. Dust the second sheet of pastry with flour and stretch it so it will lay on top of the base sheet. Push out any air from between the sheets to seal them, and cut out each of the shrimp balls with a round cookie cutter. The cookie cutter needs to be slightly larger than the space that the shrimp balls are taking up. Allow the initial brushing of egg wash to dry before the second sheet, which might have a lot of flour dusted on it, is placed over it. Place the pirozhki on a baking sheet and brush the tops with the remaining egg mixture. Chill in the refrigerator before baking. Remove and bake 12 minutes. Serve hot.

To make the béarnaise sauce, mix the egg yolks with the wine, lemon juice, and water in the top of a double boiler set over simmering water. Whip until a smooth emulsion forms. Remove from heat and continuously whip while adding the clarified butter. If sauce separates, you will have to start over. Season the sauce with the tarragon, salt, and pepper.

Place three pirozhki on each plate and pour a little sauce next to each one of them. The chef says that this is an original finger food, so no silverware is required.

Shorty's Guacamole

SHORTY'S, OWNERS BRYAN WILSON,
BRIAN HOGAN, AND MICHAEL MURPHY

Serves 6 to 8

This creative little pizza parlor with the big-screen TVs prides itself on creative takes on familiar fare, like this fresh-smashed guac, served with flatbread.

6 ripe avocados
1 large lime, quartered (room temperature is best)
1 cup Pico de Gallo (recipe follows)
¾ teaspoon kosher salt

Cut the avocados in half and remove the pits. Use a spoon to remove the flesh from the avocado. Squeeze lime juice over avocados, and then add the pico de gallo and salt. Mash the guacamole (potato masher works well) leaving some small chunks for texture. Serve immediately.

NOTES: The acidity is "brighter" if the guacamole is served immediately.

If you must prepare it in advance, place the pits on top of the guacamole to keep it from browning and cover the surface with plastic wrap.

Sardinian flatbread can be found in Italian specialty food stores and usually comes in packs of ten to twelve pieces of 12-inch razor-thin flatbreads.

Pico de Gallo

Makes about 2 cups

    1 large beefsteak tomato, diced (approximately ¾ cup)
    ½ red onion, diced (approximately ¾ cup)
    3 jalapeños, seeded and diced (approximately ¼ cup)
    ¼ bunch cilantro, chopped (approximately ¼ cup loosely packed)
    ½ cup vegetable oil
    ½ teaspoon kosher salt

    Toss all the ingredients together. Cover tightly and store in a nonreactive container.

    The pico de gallo will hold in the refrigerator for 2–3 days.

Rabbit Salad

CAKES & ALE, OWNERS BILLY AND KRISTIN ALLIN

Serves 4 as a main course, or 8–10 as a side dish

You can find pickled vegetables at your local specialty grocer. Purchase at least three different kinds of pickled vegetables (such as turnips, cauliflower, carrots, or radishes).

Rabbit

- 1 whole rabbit
- ½ (750ml) bottle fruity white wine, such as Pinot Grigio
- 1 carrot, chopped
- 1 rib celery, chopped
- 1 onion, chopped
- 2 cloves garlic, lightly crushed with the palm of your hand
- 2 bay leaves
- 3 to 4 sprigs thyme
- Water
- 3 tablespoons salt
- Freshly ground black pepper

Barley

- 2 cups faro or hulled barley
- 2 tablespoons salt
- 2 bay leaves
- Water
- 2 tablespoons olive oil

Vinaigrette

- ¼ cup olive oil
- 2 tablespoons red wine vinegar
- ½ teaspoon Dijon mustard
- Salt and freshly ground black pepper

Crème Fraîche

- ¼ cup crème fraîche
- 1 teaspoon whole-grain mustard
- 1 teaspoon milk

Salad

- Pickled vegetables, thinly sliced
- 2 green garlic stems or 2 green onions, thinly sliced
- 1 small fennel bulb, julienned and soaked in cold water for 15 minutes
- 3 tablespoons chopped fresh flat-leaf parsley
- 1 cup sunflower sprouts, watercress, or arugula

To prepare the rabbit, combine the rabbit, wine, carrot, celery, onion, garlic, bay leaves, and thyme in a large zippered plastic bag and marinate in the refrigerator for 24 hours, turning occasionally.

Preheat the oven to 300 degrees F.

Transfer the rabbit and marinade into a casserole dish. Add enough water to just cover the rabbit. Season with salt and some

pepper. Braise, covered, in the oven for 1 hour and 20 minutes, or until tender. Let it cool in the liquid (preferably overnight). Remove the meat from the bones in thumb-size chunks. Set aside. Discard the bones.

To prepare the barley, place the barley in a colander and rinse with running water until the water runs clear. Combine in a saucepan with the salt and bay leaves. Add enough water to cover. Simmer for 1 hour, or until tender. Drain. Place on a sheet pan and toss with the olive oil.

To prepare the vinaigrette, stir together the olive oil, vinegar, and mustard. Add salt and pepper to taste.

To prepare the crème fraîche, stir together the crème fraîche, mustard, and milk.

To assemble the salad, combine the rabbit, barley, pickled vegetables, green garlic, fennel, parsley, and vinaigrette and toss to mix. Add the sunflower shoots and drizzle with the crème fraîche.

North Georgia Apple & Crispy Brussels Sprout Salad

4TH & SWIFT, CHEF JAY SWIFT

Serves 4

Every fall, legions of "leaf peepers" slowly trace the North Georgia mountains' two-lane roads seeking two things: autumn color and apples. Here, local fruit is put to good use in a rich, warm fall vegetable salad.

4 cups apple cider

1 cup pistachio nuts, toasted

2 sprigs rosemary, chopped

Pinch of fleur de sel

4 cups vegetable oil, for deep-frying

25 Brussels sprouts, trimmed and halved

Salt and freshly ground black pepper

2 tablespoons sherry vinegar

1 cup crème fraîche

3 apples (preferably local and with high acidity), peeled and cut into 1 x ½-inch slices

Bring the apple cider to a boil in a small saucepan and reduce until syrupy. Cool and reserve.

Grind the pistachios to a coarse consistency by hand or in a food processor. Mix in the rosemary and fleur de sel.

Heat the oil in a tall saucepan or in deep-fryer to 350 degrees F. Fry the Brussels sprouts until outside leaves begin to turn golden brown. Do not over-fry. Remove the sprouts from fryer and drain on paper towels. Toss in bowl with salt, pepper, and vinegar.

To serve, spread some crème fraîche in a line on each plate (this will hold the sprouts in place). Liberally spread the reduced cider mixture on top of crème fraîche. Place the sprouts in a line on top of cider and crème fraîche. Top with the apples. Repeat the original process for each individual serving plate. To finish, add one last drizzle of cider reduction, then sprinkle the pistachio mix liberally over each plate.

Parmesan and Truffle Popcorn

4TH & SWIFT, CHEF JAY SWIFT

Serves 4

Jay Swift's addictive snack is this deceptively simple nosh with grated Parmesan and truffle oil, served warm in a paper cone.

1 tablespoon plus 1 teaspoon vegetable oil, divided
½ cup unpopped popcorn kernels
1 tablespoon truffle butter, melted
½ teaspoon black truffle oil
¼ cup freshly grated Parmesan cheese
Salt

Heat 1 tablespoon vegetable oil over high heat in a large pot with a tight-fitting lid. Add the popcorn and cover. Shake the pan a few times to make sure all the kernels are loose. Cook, shaking the pan occasionally while you hear the kernels pop. When the popping stops, transfer the popped corn to a large bowl.

Add the remaining vegetable oil, truffle butter, truffle oil, Parmesan, and salt to taste. Toss to coat the popcorn and serve hot.

Fried Green Tomatoes

HORSERADISH GRILL, CHEF DANIEL ALTERMAN

Serves 6 to 8

This Southern favorite started as a humble way to use up green tomatoes left on the vine after the first frost. At Horseradish Grill, the dish is a feast of flavors, with spicy pecans and goat cheese crumbles. But the green tomatoes' briskly tart taste is still front and center.

Tomatoes

- 4 cups buttermilk
- ½ teaspoon black pepper
- 1 teaspoon Tabasco Sauce
- 1 tablespoon Worcestershire sauce
- 4 green tomatoes, sliced ⅜ inch thick

Tomato Flour

- 1½ cups white cornmeal
- ¾ cup flour
- 2 tablespoons cornstarch
- 1 teaspoon cayenne pepper
- 1 teaspoon black pepper

Spicy Pecans

- 1 cup pecans, broken into pieces
- ⅛ cup butter
- 1 tablespoon pure maple syrup
- ½ teaspoon cayenne pepper
- ½ teaspoon chili powder
- 1 teaspoon flour

Remoulade Sauce

- ¾ cup olive oil
- ¼ cup lemon juice
- ¼ cup Creole mustard
- 2 tablespoons prepared horseradish
- ⅔ cup onion, finely chopped
- ⅔ cup celery, finely chopped
- ¼ cup green onions, chopped
- 2 tablespoons parsley, finely chopped
- 2 tablespoons paprika
- 1 teaspoon salt
- ⅛ teaspoon white pepper
- Dash of Tabasco Sauce
- 1 teaspoon chopped garlic
- 1 pinch cayenne pepper

To Serve

- Oil for deep-frying
- 3 tablespoons goat cheese crumbles
- 3 tablespoons remoulade sauce

To prepare the tomatoes, combine the buttermilk, black pepper, and Tabasco and Worcestershire sauces in a shallow bowl. Add the tomato slices and marinate for 1 hour.

To prepare the tomato flour, combine the cornmeal, flour,

cornstarch, cayenne, and black pepper; mix well.

Preheat the oven to 200 degrees F.

To prepare the pecans, combine the pecans, butter, maple syrup, cayenne, chili powder, and flour in a large skillet over medium heat. Sauté on very low heat until nuts begin to soften, about 20 minutes. Transfer nut mixture to an ungreased sheet pan and spread out. Bake 1½ to 2 hours, until the pecans are soft and cooked thoroughly.

To make the remoulade sauce, combine all ingredients in a blender and blend on medium speed for 5 minutes. The leftover sauce may be stored in a refrigerator for several days.

In a skillet, heat 1 inch oil for deep-frying to 350 degrees F.

Dredge the tomato slices in the tomato flour and slide into the hot oil. Fry for 1½ minutes, until golden. Drain well.

Arrange the tomato slices on a plate and sprinkle spicy pecans and goat cheese over top. Drizzle remoulade sauce over tomatoes and serve.

Cobb Salad

SUNDIAL, CHEF CHRISTIAN MESSIER

Serves 4

Atop the Westin Peachtree Plaza, the Sundial rotates to give every visitor a panoramic view of the city. Look north to Cobb County while enjoying this salad—and be careful where you set your purse. It could rotate around the room without you.

Baby field greens

1 roasted chicken breast, sliced

2 ounces cooked bacon, diced

$\frac{1}{2}$ avocado, diced

$\frac{1}{3}$ cup diced red onion

$\frac{1}{3}$ cup diced tomato

$\frac{1}{3}$ cup diced cucumber

2 ounces Maytag blue cheese, crumbled

1 hard-boiled egg, diced

Salad dressing

Line a large plate with the greens. Arrange on top the chicken, bacon, avocado, onion, tomato, cucumber, blue cheese, and egg. Lightly drizzle the salad dressing on top and serve with additional dressing on the side.

Sweetwater 420 Mussels

REPAST, CHEF JOE TRUEX

Serves 10

Husband and wife chefs Joe Truex and Mihoku Obunai combine Asian grace and simplicity with local style and ingredients—such as Atlanta's own Sweetwater 420 Ale.

5 pounds mussels, scrubbed and de-bearded

4 ounces smoked bacon, diced

1 large onion, diced

1 rib celery, diced

1 large carrot, diced

1 (12-ounce) bottle Sweetwater 420 beer

½ cup white wine

2 tablespoons butter, melted

In a large pot, soak the mussels in lightly salted cold water to cover for 10 minutes.

In a separate large pot, fry the bacon over medium-high heat until crispy. Add the onion, celery, and carrot and sauté over high heat about 3 minutes, until tender. Add the mussels, beer, and wine; cover pot and bring to a boil. Cook for 10 minutes, reduce heat to low, and continue cooking for 5 minutes, until the mussels open. Discard any unopened mussels.

Transfer the mussels to serving bowls, drizzle with butter, and serve.

Heirloom Cherry Tomato Salad with Parmesan Cookies and Strawberry Gazpacho

RITZ-CARLTON DINING ROOM,
CHEF ARNAUD BERTHELIER

Serves 4

Like the Dining Room itself, the taste of good summer tomatoes is ephemeral and transitory, specific to the season. Atlanta's most-honored restaurant is gone, but here is a taste of its elegance under chef Arnaud Berthelier.

Parmesan Cookies

- 2 cups flour
- 2¼ cups freshly grated Parmesan cheese
- ¾ cup unsalted butter, at room temperature
- 2 eggs

Strawberry Gazpacho

- 1 pint strawberries, hulled and halved
- 3 tablespoons sugar
- Balsamic vinegar

Tomatoes

- 2 pints cherry tomatoes
- 2 tablespoons chopped chives
- 1 tablespoon chopped shallot
- Salt
- Szechuan pepper
- Sugar
- 2 cups watermelon, seeded and diced, to garnish

Preheat the oven to 300 degrees F. Line a sheet pan with parchment paper.

In a food processor, combine the flour and Parmesan and pulse to mix together.

In an electric mixer fitted with a paddle attachment, whip the butter until creamy. Add the eggs and mix at low speed for 1 minute. Add the flour mixture and mix on low speed until fully incorporated; do not over-mix.

On a lightly floured surface, roll out the dough to a ¼- to ⅛-inch thickness. If the dough is difficult to handle, chill briefly and then roll out. Cut to any desired shape. Bake for 12 minutes, until

lightly browned. Let cool.

To prepare the gazpacho, combine the strawberries and sugar in a blender and process until smooth. Add balsamic vinegar to taste. Strain and chill until you are ready to serve.

To prepare the tomato salad, blanch the tomatoes for 30 seconds in boiling water. Immediately transfer to ice water to stop the cooking. Drain and peel off the skin.

Combine tomatoes in a bowl with the chives and shallots. Sprinkle with salt, Szechuan pepper, and sugar to taste.

To serve, place a cookie on each plate. Top with the tomato salad. Drizzle the gazpacho around. Garnish with small dices of watermelon.

Boiled Peanuts

DAVID'S PRODUCE, OWNER DAVID GLENN

Serves 5

Think of these hot legumes as the South's answer to edamame, the green boiled soybean you find in Japanese restaurants. And if you remember them as mushy, try them again—they're best when freshly cooked and still just a little "al dente."

3 pounds Valencia or Jumbo peanuts (the best are usually found from roadside vendors)

$\frac{1}{3}$ to $\frac{1}{2}$ cup salt

Water to cover

Combine the peanuts and salt in a stockpot and fill with water until the peanuts are covered. Bring to a boil over high heat and cook, keeping an eye on the water level. Add more water as it boils out. It takes 2–3 hours for the peanuts to cook, and you have to keep an eye on them and taste them until they are ready. Drain. Any extras can be refrigerated for up to 5 or 6 days. They are also good served cold.

You can also freeze and then microwave for a couple of minutes if you would like to serve them warm.

Melocoton, or Tomato and Peach Salad with Serrano Ham
CUERNO

Serves 6

Owner Riccardo Ullio's other, better-known restaurants (Fritti and Sotto Sotto) focus on Italian fare. Cuerno, now closed, was one of Atlanta's first serious Spanish restaurants, with authentic tapas and paellas.

3 heirloom tomatoes, cut into wedges

3 ripe peaches, cut into wedges

1 red onion, thinly sliced

¼ pound Serrano ham, torn into strips

¼ cup coarsely chopped fresh flat-leaf parsley

1 tablespoon chopped fresh oregano

2 tablespoons sherry vinegar

¼ cup extra virgin olive oil

Salt and freshly ground black pepper

Combine the tomatoes, peaches, onion, ham, parsley, and oregano in a serving bowl. Dress with the vinegar and olive oil and season to taste with salt and pepper. Serve chilled.

Macaroni and Cheese

Mary Mac's Tea Room

Comfort Foods
Culinary Analgesics

S. R. Henrietta Dull's landmark 1928 book, *Southern Cooking*, includes many familiar chapters—"Milk and Cheese," "Meats," "Salads"—and one or two unusual ones, such as "Pickles" and "Fritters," as well as another section that was then common: "Invalid Dishes." You may not recognize the old-fashioned word—and no, we're not talking about the synonym for "not valid"—meaning a convalescent shut-in. If wives and mothers didn't have enough work and worry, they usually also had to care for whoever was ill—and with extended families living under one roof, that meant a whole other menu just about every day. With directions on how to squeeze the juice from a steak or soft-cook an egg in a teacup, Mrs. Dull's "invalid" dishes are aimed at the slow-recovering child or adult with a sensitive stomach. Fortunately, modern medicine means that most homes don't contain invalids anymore. However, we all still have down days when only a certain kind of comfort food can make it all right again. Typically, we prefer to be coaxed gently into a good mood with subtle, familiar flavors (preferably in a velvety texture) from our childhood—you rarely want to be jolted out of a funk with hot spices or startling combinations. Familiar soups and sandwiches often fit the bill, because they are usually friendly on the tongue, kind on the stomach, and high on nostalgia.

Roasted Vidalia Onion Soup with Cornmeal Griddle Cakes and White Cheddar

DOGWOOD, CHEF SHANE TOUHY

Serves 10 to 12

Georgia's favorite sweet onion melts into this subtly layered soup, topped with sharp white cheddar and a crisp griddle cake.

3 Vidalia or other sweet onions, peeled and left whole

2 cloves garlic, peeled and left whole

12 cups chicken stock or broth

3½ cups heavy cream

2 tablespoons Harvey's Bristol Cream or other good cream sherry

1 tablespoon kosher salt

½ teaspoon ground white pepper

4 ounces white cheddar cheese, grated

Cornmeal Griddle Cakes

½ cup flour

½ cup cornmeal

2¼ teaspoons sugar

¾ teaspoon baking powder

1½ teaspoons salt

Pinch of ground white pepper

1 large egg

6 tablespoons buttermilk

2 tablespoons half-and-half

2 tablespoons very thinly sliced scallion or green onion

¼ cup olive oil

Preheat the oven to 325 degrees F.

Wrap the whole onions and garlic together in heavy-duty aluminum foil. Roast the onions and garlic for 45 minutes. Unwrap and allow to cool slightly, until you are able to handle them. Cut the onions in quarters. Combine the onions, garlic, and the stock in a stockpot and bring to a boil. Turn the heat down to a simmer and continue to cook for approximately 30 minutes, until reduced by one-quarter.

Meanwhile, prepare the griddle cakes. In a mixing bowl, combine the flour, cornmeal, sugar, baking powder, salt, and white pepper. Set aside.

In another mixing bowl, whisk together the egg, buttermilk, and half-and-half until smooth. Combine the wet and dry mixtures together, and fold in the scallion.

Heat the olive oil on a griddle or in a shallow sauté pan over medium

heat. Spoon about 2 tablespoons of the mixture into the pan. Brown on both sides, about 2 to 3 minutes a side. Repeat to make ten to twelve griddle cakes. Keep warm.

When the soup has reduced, puree in batches in a blender until smooth. Transfer to a large bowl or another pot. Add the heavy cream, sherry, salt, and pepper, and stir until completely blended.

To serve, ladle the soup into bowls. Top each bowl of soup with a griddle cake and a sprinkling of cheese.

South Georgia Salmon Croquettes

THE PECAN, CHEF/OWNER TONY MORROW

Makes 20 croquettes

Was there ever a more beloved Depression-era food than salmon croquettes? Somehow, Southern luncheonettes made a delicacy from canned fish, crackers or bread crumbs, and a white sauce. The Pecan's version uses flour, cornmeal, and hollandaise.

Salmon

2 (14-ounce) cans salmon, drained

8 large eggs, lightly beaten

1 cup flour

1 cup cornmeal

1 onion, chopped

Juice of 1 lemon

Salt and freshly ground black pepper

2 tablespoons butter, plus more as needed

Hollandaise Sauce

$1/2$ cup butter

2 egg yolks, well beaten

$1/4$ teaspoon salt

Pinch cayenne pepper

1 tablespoon freshly squeezed lemon juice

To prepare the croquettes, first remove the bones from the salmon. Mix together the salmon, eggs, flour, cornmeal, and onion in a mixing bowl. Add the lemon juice and salt and pepper to taste. Form into 4-ounce patties, 4 inches in diameter and $1/4$ inch thick.

To cook the croquettes, melt the butter in a nonstick skillet over medium heat. Add as many croquettes as will fit without crowding in the pan. Cook until golden on both sides, about 2 minutes per side. Remove and keep warm. Cook the remaining croquettes, adding more butter as needed. Keep warm while you prepare the sauce.

To prepare the hollandaise sauce, divide the butter into three portions. Combine the egg yolks with one-third of the butter in top of double boiler over hot (not boiling) water. Beating constantly with a wire whisk, add another portion of butter when the first butter melts. Continue to beat and, when the butter is melting, add the

remaining butter and continue beating as the butter melts and the mixture thickens. Remove from heat and add the salt, cayenne, and lemon juice. (If the sauce separates, beat in 2 tablespoons boiling water drop by drop.)

Serve the croquettes with the hollandaise sauce.

Pork Belly Torta

HOLY TACO, CHEF/OWNER ROBERT PHALEN

Makes 5 to 6 sandwiches

At this happening little East Atlanta Village spot, the Mexican sandwich called a torta—typically served with tomato, onion, and a slice of avocado—is a decidedly jazzed-up version, using the unctuous Southern favorite, pork belly, on ciabatta bread.

4 pounds fresh pork belly

Salt and freshly ground
    black pepper

1 large yellow onion, chopped

2 carrots, chopped

3 celery stalks, chopped

½ cup tomato paste

4 cloves garlic

2 bay leaves

10 black peppercorns

8 cups chicken stock, or
    enough
    to cover meat

For each sandwich

10 to 12 ounces high-
    quality ciabatta, or 2
    ounces ciabatta per
    sandwich, cut in half

Mayonnaise to taste

Monterey Jack cheese,
    grated or sliced thin

Sliced plum tomatoes

Lettuce leaves

Pickled jalapeño slices

Sliced onions

Sliced radishes

Preheat the oven to 350 degrees F.

To prepare the pork, season generously with salt and pepper. Heat a large skillet over high heat. Add the meat and sear for 15 minutes until golden brown all around. Remove the meat from the pan and keep warm. Add the onion, carrots, and celery and sauté until golden, about 5 minutes. Add the tomato paste, garlic, bay leaves, and peppercorns. Cook a few minutes more.

Place the pork in a roasting pan. Add the mixture from the skillet, cover with chicken stock, and then cover with aluminum foil. Roast for 2½ hours, or until pork is fork tender. Remove pork from the roasting pan and cool. Discard the vegetables and pan juices. This can all be done a day in advance.

Preheat the oven to 350 degrees F.

To prepare each sandwich, slice the cooled pork into 1-inch-thick

slices. Season the meat with salt. Heat a sauté pan over high heat. Add the meat slice and cook about 6 minutes on each side until crispy, turning once. Slice the bread and toast in the oven. Cover the bread with mayonnaise, then with a layer of cheese. Return to the oven for 1 minute, or until the cheese is melted. Build the sandwich with the meat, tomatoes, lettuce, jalapeños, onions, and radishes. Serve immediately.

Truffled White Bean Soup

FRENCH AMERICAN BRASSERIE,
CHEF STEVE SHARP

Serves 6 to 8

Whoever heard of an elegant bean soup? FAB, of course, in a pureed version that calls for truffle oil and a thick slice of baguette.

4 cups dried white beans, such as great Northern beans

2 tablespoons grapeseed oil, for frying bacon

8 ounces smoked bacon, diced

8 cloves garlic, chopped

2 inner white celery ribs, chopped

1 large carrot, chopped

1 large yellow onion, chopped

4 sprigs thyme

2 sprigs fresh rosemary

2 bay leaves

4 quarts chicken stock, plus more as needed

4 cups heavy cream, plus more as needed

Salt and white pepper

2 ounces truffle oil, for drizzling

Warmed bread, to serve

Soak the beans in 12 cups water for 24 hours, then drain.

Heat the grapeseed oil in a large pot over medium heat. Fry the bacon for 10 minutes, or until brown. Add the garlic and lightly toast, being careful not to burn because it can make the soup bitter. Add the celery, carrots, and onion and sauté for about 10 minutes, until softened but not colored. Add the thyme, rosemary, bay leaves, chicken stock, and beans. Simmer until the beans are cooked through and soft, about 1½ to 2 hours, or until the beans pop.

Add the cream, increase the heat to medium-high, and cook for 10 minutes.

Puree with a hand blender (or puree in batches in a standing blender). Season with salt and white pepper. Make sure the puree is a consistency pleasing to you. If you want a thicker soup, you can reduce the soup slowly. If it is too thick, add more stock and cream to thin it out.

To serve, ladle the soup into warm bowls, drizzle with truffle oil, and serve with warm bread.

Croque Monsieur

JOËL BRASSERIE, CHEF CYRILLE HOLATA

Serves 4

Oh, it may sound as fancy as this French restaurant's sleek dining room—but the croque monsieur is nothing more than a luxurious Gallic ham-and-cheese sandwich. At Joël Brasserie, it is baked in béchamel sauce.

6 tablespoons butter

⅔ cup flour

2 cups milk, plus more as needed

1 pinch salt

1 pinch freshly ground black pepper

1 pinch grated nutmeg

8 slices from large loaf fresh French country bread

8 slices ham

8 ounces Gruyère or Swiss cheese, sliced thin

Preheat the oven to 350 degrees F.

Melt the butter in a small saucepan over medium heat. Add the flour, stirring to form a smooth paste. Cook briefly. Stir in the milk. The sauce will thicken; stir well. Add the salt, pepper, and nutmeg and continue to cook for 4 to 5 minutes, until thickened and smooth. To test the thickness of the sauce, dip a finger into a spoonful of the sauce. If the sauce sticks to the finger it is too thick; if a line doesn't form it is too thin; if a line forms without sticking to the finger it is perfect. If it is too thick, add additional milk.

Toast the bread. Spread sauce on four of the slices, lay two slices of ham and two ounces of the cheese on each. Top with more sauce. Close the sandwiches with the remaining bread. Place in a baking dish large enough to hold the sandwiches in a single layer. On top of the sandwiches, spread the remaining sauce.

Bake for 6 to 10 minutes. Serve hot.

Macaroni and Cheese

MARY MAC'S TEA ROOM, OWNER JOHN FERRELL

Serves 6 to 8

Chances are, when you look into Mary Mac's, at least half the folks there are having fried chicken. But probably two-thirds have picked this custardy, cheese-crusted casserole as one of their sides.

1 cup macaroni

3 large eggs

2 cups whole milk

$\frac{1}{2}$ teaspoon freshly ground white pepper

2 tablespoons butter, melted

$\frac{1}{2}$ teaspoon salt

1 teaspoon hot sauce

2 cups grated extra-sharp cheddar cheese

Paprika

Preheat the oven to 350 degrees F. Butter an 8-inch square baking dish.

Bring a pot of salted water to a boil. Add the macaroni, stir well, and simmer for 10 minutes. Pour into colander and rinse. Drain until almost dry.

In a medium bowl, beat the eggs until light yellow. Add the milk, white pepper, butter, salt, and hot sauce and mix well.

Put a layer of cooked macaroni in the prepared baking dish. Add a layer of the egg mixture, then a layer of the cheese. Repeat the layers, ending with cheese on top. Dust with paprika.

Bake for 35–40 minutes, or until the custard is set. Serve hot.

See page 54 for picture.

Tunisian Spicy Tuna Sandwich

ALON'S BAKERY, OWNER ALON BALSHAN

Makes 1 sandwich

Alon's is best known for its artisan breads and pastries, but the bakery also makes fantastic sandwiches, perfect for Chastain Park concerts.

1 (8-ounce) can albacore tuna

2 tablespoons capers

2 tablespoons finely chopped parsley

3 tablespoons freshly squeezed lemon juice

1 tablespoon chopped preserved lemons

2 tablespoons extra virgin olive oil

Salt and pepper to taste

1 hard-boiled egg, sliced

1 small Yukon gold potato, cubed and boiled

Demi baguette

Harissa sauce (North African hot sauce, sold in Middle Eastern shops and online)

Mix tuna, capers, parsley, lemon juice, preserved lemons, olive oil, and salt and pepper to taste. The salad should be moist from the lemon juice and olive oil, with a taste of acidity from the lemon juice. You can always add more olive oil and lemon juice to taste. Carefully fold in the sliced hard-boiled egg and potatoes.

Slice the demi baguette and remove the soft center part of the bread. Spread with harissa sauce to your liking, stuff it with the tuna salad, and bon appétit!

Grilled Shrimp
on Sugar Cane

NAM, OWNERS CHRIS AND ALEX KINJO

Serves 2

In Atlanta's best Vietnamese restaurant, the shrimp ball is grilled on sugar cane. After you've finished with the shrimp, you chew on the sugar cane. It's a dish with a built-in dessert.

1½ ounces pork belly, minced

3 ounces shrimp, peeled and deveined

½ teaspoon salt

½ teaspoon black pepper

1 tablespoon canola oil

1 teaspoon cornstarch

1 (4-inch) piece fresh sugar cane

Combine the pork belly and shrimp in a food processor and process until mixed thoroughly. Add the salt and pepper, oil, and cornstarch and pulse until blended.

Shave off the sugar cane skin. Cut the length of the sugar cane in half and then in half again until you have four pieces; cut in quarters lengthwise. Wrap the shrimp blend around the sugar cane pieces to a thickness of about ¼ inch.

Grill on a lightly oiled grill on low to medium heat for approximately 5 minutes, turning frequently until a golden brown.

Chicken Noodle Soup
with Kreplach

GOLDBERG'S DELI, CHEF/ OWNER WAYNE SAXE

Serves 6 to 8

What could make you feel better than chicken soup? How about chicken noodle soup with kreplach, the delicious meaty dumpling? It couldn't hurt!

Soup

1 medium onion, finely diced

2 tablespoons schmaltz (rendered chicken fat, available at most stores)

1 (3-pound) whole chicken

1 rib celery, finely diced

2 carrots, medium dice or cut into coins

1/2 cup chicken stock

Pinch white pepper

3/4 pound wide egg noodles, cooked according to directions, drained

Cook diced onions in schmaltz until dark brown, about 5 minutes.

Place whole chicken in pot of water to cover. Add celery, carrots, and browned onions to the pot and bring everything to a boil. Continue to simmer over medium heat until vegetables are tender, about 35 to 45 minutes. Remove the whole chicken from the pot and peel off the skin. Pull pieces of chicken off the bone and put them back in the pot. Add the chicken stock and white pepper and simmer for 15 minutes. After 15 minutes, add noodles to pot.

This soup is best when prepared one day and served the next.

Kreplach

Makes 16

2 pounds ground chuck

1 medium onion, finely diced

2 tablespoons schmaltz

1 package (4-inch squares) wonton wrappers

Pinch salt

Pinch pepper

While the soup is simmering, fry the ground chuck in a large skillet. Do not add fat. Fry onions in schmaltz over medium heat until brown, about 5 minutes. Mix ground chuck and onions and

let the mixture cool. Place a small amount of the mixture onto a wonton wrapper and fold the wrapper into a rectangular or triangular shape. Using the tines of a fork, press the edges of the wrapper (kreplach). Add the kreplach to the soup after the noodles are added and cook the soup on low for 2 to 3 minutes. Serve soup hot, with two kreplach per bowl.

Cuban Sandwich

SAWICKI'S GROCERY,
CHEF/OWNER LYNNE SAWICKI

Serves 1

If you're old enough to remember the old Dagwood comic strip, you can appreciate this little-bit-of-everything-good sandwich, with ham and pork, cheese and beef, pressed and grilled (perfect if you have an indoor grill, panini maker, or even just something you can mash it into the skillet with).

1 tablespoon whole-grain mustard

1 hoagie roll, split lengthwise

1 tablespoon mojo vinaigrette, citrus vinaigrette,
  or any tart salad dressing

4 slices spicy bread-and-butter pickles

1 ounce Swiss cheese, thinly sliced

2 ounces Black Forest ham, thinly sliced

3 ounces roasted pork loin, thinly sliced

1 teaspoon honey butter

Spread the mustard on one side of the roll, and drizzle the vinaigrette on the other side. Lay the pickles on the side with the mustard, then split the Swiss between both sides of the roll and close.

In a pan or griddle, warm the ham and pork loin at medium heat. Set aside but keep warm. Spread the honey butter on the outsides of the roll and brown each side in the pan. Open the roll, add the pork loin and ham, cut in half, and enjoy!

Mom's Cabbage Soup

NAM, OWNERS CHRIS AND ALEX KINJO

Serves 2

Young restaurateurs Chris and Alex Kinjo have three of the hippest restaurants in town (MF Sushibar, Nam, and MF Buckhead), but in Nam's kitchen, their mom is in charge.

1 ounce dried wood ear mushrooms

2 large regular green cabbage leaves

2 to 3 scallions, green part only

1 ounce shrimp, peeled and deveined

2 to 3 teaspoons Blue claw crabmeat (not imitation)

3 cups chicken or seafood soup stock

Chopped fresh cilantro

1 tablespoon Asian fish sauce

Pinch salt

Pinch sugar

Soak the mushrooms in warm water to cover for 30 minutes. Drain well.

Steam or boil the cabbage leaf and scallions for 15 minutes, or until soft enough to bend and fold. Cut four equal-sided 3-inch triangles from the cabbage leaf.

Combine the shrimp, crab, and mushrooms in a food processor and process until well blended. Place a teaspoon of the shrimp mix onto each cabbage piece. Roll into a dumpling by gathering the edges to form a purse. Tie the dumpling using the steamed scallions. There will be 4 dumplings per person, so cut the scallions accordingly.

Bring the soup stock to a boil in a medium saucepan. Add the dumplings and cilantro. Return to a boil and skim off any impurities on the surface. Add the fish sauce, salt, and sugar. Use a light boil for 15 to 20 minutes to further cook the soup. Serve hot.

Diver Scallop Benedict
Rathbun's

Fish & Seafood
Swim Club

Georgia is blessed with finned and shelled fare from its Atlantic coastline, mountain streams, and deep freshwater lakes and reservoirs. More fortuitously, Atlanta boasts a wide range of cultures, with cooks who all approach it differently. But the more these cultural approaches differ, the more we find they are the same as ours: whether using a refined Continental methodology or gutsy peasant style, each chef coaxes the best out of his native aquatic offerings, sealing in subtle tastes by sautéing or gently steaming, and then rounding out the flavors with a little ecosystem of local herbs and vegetables.

The following recipes are an around-the-world tour, including stops in Bangkok, Montego Bay, Paris, Madrid, and Rome. Of course, you're always going to have to change planes in Atlanta. We couldn't supply less than two recipes for our town's favorite brunch dish—shrimp and grits—and one for the star of our Saturday night fish fries—catfish.

Corn Milk–Poached Maine Lobster Tail with Gratin of Mustard and Blood Orange Reduction

EUGENE, CHEF/OWNER LINTON HOPKINS

Serves 4

Native son Linton Hopkins "Southernizes" this Yankee lobster with sweet corn milk in this thoroughly modern restaurant named for his grandfather.

Lobster

4 Maine lobsters, 1½ pounds each

6 ears sweet corn

Gratin of Mustard

6 tablespoons whole-grain mustard

1 large egg yolk

Blood Orange Reduction

3 blood oranges

Chives, chopped as garnish

To prepare the lobster, bring a large pot of water to a boil. Add the lobsters and blanch for 3 minutes. Remove and plunge into ice water immediately. When the lobsters are cold, remove tail from body. Reserve the claws and body for alternate use. Peel the shell off the tail and reserve the meat.

Cut the kernels off the corn cob and scrape all the juice out of cob. Push all through a juicer. If you don't have a juicer, the corn can be pureed and strained; the finer the grain of the puree the more flavor the juice will have. Reserve the juice and discard the solids. Fully cover the lobster meat with the juice, then heat to 175 degrees F and hold until you are ready to serve.

To prepare the mustard gratin, mix the mustard with the egg yolk. Spoon one quarter onto each plate and create a thin circle.

Caramelize with a blowtorch or under a broiler; reserve.

To prepare the reduction, juice two of the oranges. Boil the juice until it is reduced to the consistency of a syrup. Peel the remaining orange and separate into segments.

To plate, place the lobster onto the circle of mustard and arrange the blood orange segments. Place the oranges at the highest point of the plate and let them fall naturally into place, then spoon the reduced blood orange syrup around the plate. Garnish with chives.

Snapper Escovich

KOOL RUNNINGS, OWNER TONY REID

Serves 6

The longtime Memorial Drive Jamaican destination features one of the island's signature dishes: escovitch, a fried fish topped with a hot vinegar dressing—perhaps derived from the tropical citrus-marinated raw seafood dish, ceviche.

6 whole small to medium (¼ to ½ pound) snappers, cleaned, head and tail left on

¼ cup white vinegar, divided

1½ teaspoons salt

1½ teaspoons black pepper

Vegetable oil, for frying

3 cloves garlic, divided

2 onions, sliced

2 Scotch bonnet peppers, seeded and sliced

10 whole pimentos, fresh or bottled

Wash fish in ⅛ cup white vinegar and water. Pat dry and place on a plate. Cut small deep slits on each side of the fish. Rub salt and pepper on the outside, in the slits, and on the inside.

Heat ¼ inch oil in the skillet and sauté 2 cloves garlic over high heat; remove from the skillet when they begin to color. Carefully place the fish in the hot oil, adding as many pieces as the frying pan will hold. Fry the fish on high heat for about 5 minutes until crisp, turning down the heat when the fish starts steaming. Turn the fish over and fry the opposite side on medium heat until crisp and brown, about 6 minutes. Transfer the fried fish to paper towels to drain. Fry the remaining fish in the same oil and drain.

Combine the onion, peppers, remaining clove garlic, and pimentos in a small nonreactive saucepan with the remaining vinegar. Bring to a boil and boil for about 5 minutes. (Be careful of the steam, which could cause your eyes to burn). Pour the vinegar mixture on the fried fish. Let the fish cool in the marinade before serving.

Diver Scallop Benedict

RATHBUN'S, OWNERS KEVIN RATHBUN,
CLIFFORD BRAMBLE, AND KIRK PARKS

Serves 4

Former Iron Chef champion Kevin Rathbun's namesake restaurant offers a cook's tour of regional American favorites—some with trademark twists, like this new take on a brunch classic.

Grits

- 1 tablespoon olive oil
- 3 ounces country ham, finely diced
- 2 cups stone-ground grits
- 3 cups water
- 3 cups heavy cream
- 1 teaspoon kosher salt
- ½ teaspoon black pepper

Hollandaise

- 2 large egg yolks
- 2 teaspoons freshly squeezed lemon juice
- 1 tablespoon hot water, plus more as needed
- 1½ cups clarified butter
- 1 teaspoon crushed red pepper flakes
- 1 teaspoon kosher salt
- Black pepper to taste
- 1 teaspoon Tabasco Sauce

Asparagus

- 12 asparagus spears
- 1 tablespoon extra virgin olive oil
- 2 teaspoons freshly squeezed lemon juice
- 1 teaspoon honey
- ½ teaspoon finely grated lemon zest
- ½ teaspoon kosher salt

Scallops

- 2 tablespoons olive oil
- 12 large sea scallops (U/10 diver scallops)
- 2 teaspoons kosher salt
- ½ teaspoon black pepper

To prepare the grits, heat the oil in a heavy saucepan over medium-high heat. Add the ham and sauté for 3 minutes. Add the grits, water, and cream; bring to a boil. Decrease the heat and simmer for about 40 minutes, until the grits are thick and fully cooked. Season with

continued on page 79

salt and pepper and keep warm.

To prepare the hollandaise, combine the egg yolks, lemon juice, and water in the top of a double boiler over boiling water. Whisk vigorously until the eggs are frothy.

Remove from the heat and begin adding the butter 1 tablespoon at a time, until all butter is incorporated. If mixture begins to get too thick, add a little more hot water. Add the red pepper flakes, salt, pepper, and Tabasco and keep warm.

To prepare the asparagus, bring a large pot of salted water to a boil. Add the asparagus and blanch until al dente, about 2 minutes. Transfer to an ice bath to stop the cooking.

In a small bowl, combine the olive oil, lemon juice, honey, lemon zest, and salt. Cut the asparagus on the bias into 1-inch lengths and mix with the vinaigrette.

To prepare the scallops, in a large sauté pan (cast-iron preferred) heat the olive oil over high heat. Season the scallops generously with salt and pepper and sauté for 2 to 3 minutes on each side, until golden brown.

To serve, place ½ cup grits in the middle of each plate. Circle the grits with 4 scallops and drizzle with the hollandaise. Place one-quarter of the marinated asparagus on top of the grits and serve.

Paella Valenciana

CUERNO

Serves 2 to 4

Cuerno served Spain's signature dish, paella, in many variations. This version is named for the region that embraces the dish as a part of its cultural identity.

Spanish Sofrito

- 1 tablespoon olive oil
- 2/3 cup diced onion
- 2½ tablespoons minced garlic
- ½ cinnamon stick
- 1½ cups peeled and diced tomatoes
- ½ teaspoon smoked paprika
- Small pinch saffron
- ½ teaspoon sugar

Valenciana

- 2 tablespoons olive oil
- 4 rabbit pieces (leg and thigh meat)
- 2 chicken pieces (leg and thigh with skin on)
- 1¼ cups Calasparra rice
- 30 fluid ounces seafood stock made with crab
- 7 ounces cuttlefish
- 4 canned artichoke hearts
- 2 ounces uncooked green beans, sautéed lightly until tender (approximately 3–5 minutes) on medium heat
- 4 shrimp, peeled and deveined
- 6 mussels
- 1 teaspoon saffron

Preheat the oven to 350 degrees F.

Heat the oil in a large skillet over medium-high heat. Add the onion and garlic; sauté until onion is translucent, about 3 minutes. Add the cinnamon, tomatoes, paprika, saffron, and sugar. Cook down until the mixture is thick and has an almost paste-like consistency.

To make the paella, heat the oil over medium-high heat in a paella pan or large skillet. Add the rabbit and chicken, in batches if necessary, and sauté 5 to 10 minutes, until browned on both sides. Remove from the heat and keep warm. Stir in the sofrito, then add the rice and sauté until coated in oil and translucent. Add the stock and bring to a boil. Then add the remaining ingredients. Bring to a lively simmer and cook on top of the stove for 8 minutes.

Finish in the oven for 12 minutes, uncovered.

Butter-Poached Shrimp and Grits

REPAST, CHEF JOE TRUEX

Serves 4

Shrimp and grits. Asian and Southern. Mihoku Obanai and Joe Truex. Great marriages are sometimes made in the kitchen—as this husband-and-wife cooking team demonstrate every night. In this old-school dish, shrimp's gentle flavors are courted by slow poaching in clarified butter, before joining as one with the South's favorite breakfast starch. Bacon and eggs stand by as best man and matron of honor.

3 pounds plus ¼ cup butter, divided

1½ cups stock (shrimp, chicken, or vegetable)

1 pound large shrimp, peeled and deveined (reserve the shells)

1 cup heavy cream

2 cups water

Salt and freshly ground black pepper

1 cup stone-ground grits

2 cloves garlic

2 sprigs thyme

8 slices bacon

1 tablespoon vinegar

4 large eggs

1 tablespoon lemon juice, freshly squeezed

1 lemon, juiced

Heat 3 pounds butter in a medium saucepan over medium heat to clarify. As the butter melts, the milk solids settle to the bottom of the pan. Skim off the foam. Simmer until all the water has evaporated. Pour off the clarified butter, leaving the milk solids behind in the pan.

Heat the stock in a small saucepan and set aside.

To flavor the stock, place the shrimp shells in a saucepan and cover with water. Simmer over low heat for 7 to 10 minutes, until the shells are no longer translucent. Remove from the heat and strain the broth, discarding the shells. Add this broth to the hot stock.

In a large saucepan over medium-high heat, combine the cream,

continued on page 83

water, and the hot stock; bring to a gentle boil. Add the remaining butter, salt, and pepper to taste. Slowly add the grits, stirring constantly so that the grits do not settle to the bottom and scorch. When all the grits are added, reduce the heat to medium-low and cook for 35 to 45 minutes, stirring occasionally, until the grits have absorbed all the liquid and become soft, with the same consistency as oatmeal. If the grits become too thick, add warm stock or water to thin. Remove from heat.

Sprinkle the shrimp with salt and pepper. Heat the clarified butter to 170 degrees F and add garlic and thyme. Add the shrimp and poach 5 to 7 minutes over low heat, until cooked through. Remove the shrimp with a slotted spoon. Keep warm.

Cook the bacon in a frying pan over medium heat until crisp, about 8 minutes. Drain on paper towels.

To poach the eggs, bring 3 to 4 inches of water almost to boiling. Add vinegar. One at a time, crack the eggs into a small cup and slide the egg into the water. Cook until the whites are set and the centers are soft.

To serve, spoon hot grits onto individual serving plates and top with the shrimp mixture. Drizzle with butter from poaching the shrimp and sprinkle with lemon juice. Place a poached egg on top of the grits along with 2 slices of bacon and serve immediately.

Spaghetti alla Vongole

SOTTO SOTTO, OWNER RICCARDO ULLIO

Serves 4

Sometimes the simplest flavors are best, such as pasta with olive oil, garlic, tomatoes, and small fresh clams.

Sea salt

1/2 cup extra virgin olive oil

2 cloves garlic, thinly sliced

4 dozen small clams, manila, or Italian vongole

4 cups diced tomatoes, preferably organically grown ripe heirloom tomatoes

2 tablespoons chopped fresh parsley

1 pound dried spaghetti

Bring a large pot of water to a boil. Enough sea salt should be added until the water tastes like the sea.

In a sauté pan, heat the olive oil and garlic over medium heat and cook 2–3 minutes, until garlic is translucent. Add the clams and tomatoes, cover, and cook until the clams open. Add the parsley.

Add the spaghetti to boiling water and cook the spaghetti until al dente. Drain well.

Toss the spaghetti with the clam and tomato mix. Serve immediately.

Catfish with Green Tomato Ragout

WISTERIA, CHEF JASON HILL

Serves 4

Forgetting the taste of good fried catfish is something like forgetting you're Southern. Take a bite and remember.

2 cups yellow cornmeal

1 cup flour

2 tablespoons sweet
Spanish paprika

2 tablespoons salt

2 teaspoons white pepper

1/4 teaspoon cayenne pepper

Buttermilk

Vegetable oil, for frying

16 ounces catfish fillets,
cut into 1-inch strips

Green Tomato Ragout

4 tablespoons vegetable oil

2 tablespoons butter

4 green tomatoes, diced

1 onion, diced

2 large beefsteak tomatoes,
diced (or substitute
2 small tomatoes)

2 red bell peppers, diced

2 poblano peppers,
seeded and diced

2 teaspoons Old Bay
Seafood Seasoning

Pinch dried red pepper flakes

Pinch kosher salt

Pinch white pepper

2 tablespoons minced fresh
herbs (parsley, sage,
thyme, and rosemary,
in equal proportions)

2 tablespoons minced garlic

2 shallots, minced

1/3 pound cleaned crawfish
tails, shrimp, or catfish

To make the breading, combine the cornmeal, flour, paprika, salt, white pepper, and cayenne pepper in a shallow bowl. Fill a second shallow bowl with buttermilk.

Fill a cast-iron skillet with 1 inch vegetable oil and heat to 325 degrees F. Dip the catfish strips into the buttermilk and drain off excess. Then dredge in the cornmeal breading and shake off extra

breading. Carefully place the catfish in the skillet and fry until golden brown, turning once about halfway through, after 2½–3 minutes. Drain on paper towels and serve hot with Green Tomato Ragout.

Heat the oil and butter in a large saucepan over medium-high heat. Add the green tomatoes, onion, beefsteak tomatoes, bell pepper, and poblano pepper; sauté 4–5 minutes, or until onions are translucent. Add the Old Bay Seasoning, red pepper flakes, salt, white pepper, herbs, garlic, and shallot. When the onions are translucent, add the catfish and simmer until warmed, about 3 minutes.

Peanut-Crusted Grouper, Baby Bok Choy, and Massaman Curry

BLUEPOINTE, BUCKHEAD LIFE
RESTAURANT GROUP

Serves 8

Massaman Curry is often made with cashews, but Bluepointe instead incorporates a Georgia legume: peanuts.

Massaman Curry

1 tablespoon vegetable oil

$\frac{1}{2}$ cup Massaman curry paste

2 teaspoons curry powder

$2\frac{1}{2}$ cups coconut milk

1 whole star anise, lightly toasted

3 cardamom pods, lightly toasted

$\frac{1}{2}$ cinnamon stick, lightly toasted

2 tablespoons palm sugar or jaggery

1 tablespoon tamarind juice (see note on facing page)

$1\frac{1}{2}$ tablespoons Asian fish sauce

Grouper

8 (6-ounce) skinless grouper fillets

$1\frac{1}{2}$ teaspoons finely ground
   sea salt

3 tablespoons unsalted butter, at
   room temperature

1 cup peanuts, shelled, lightly toasted, and crushed

$\frac{1}{2}$ cup vegetable oil

Baby Bok Choy

2 tablespoons unsalted butter

6 heads baby bok choy, trimmed

2 teaspoons finely ground sea salt

$\frac{1}{4}$ teaspoon ground white pepper

To prepare the curry, heat the oil in a saucepan over medium heat. Add the Massaman curry paste and sauté for 2 minutes. Add the curry powder. Whisk in the coconut milk and bring just to a simmer. Remove from the heat and stir in the star anise, cardamom pods, cinnamon stick, palm sugar, tamarind juice, and fish sauce. Allow the spices to infuse for 10 minutes, then strain through a fine-mesh sieve and discard the spices. Keep warm.

Preheat the oven to 400 degrees F.

To prepare the grouper, season the fillets with salt, brush the top of each fillet with butter, then place them butter-side down on the crushed peanuts.

Heat the oil in a large ovenproof skillet over medium heat. Put the fillets in the pan in a single layer, peanut-side up, and cook for 3 minutes. Transfer to the oven and roast for two minutes until the peanuts are browned; do not flip the fillets.

To prepare the bok choy, heat a skillet over medium heat, add the butter and then the bok choy. Sauté for 3 to 4 minutes, or until just tender. Season with the salt and white pepper. Keep warm.

To serve, lay a bed of bok choy onto the plate and place the fish on top of it. Spread the curry around the fish.

NOTE: To make tamarind juice, soak 1 tablespoon tamarind pulp in ¼ cup hot water, then strain and press on the solids to extract the juice.

Fried Chicken
Son's Place

Poultry
The Gospel Bird

For many Southerners, it was always a religious experience. Sunday meant fried chicken just as surely as Monday meant washing or Tuesday meant Rotary Club lunch. With a little flour, shortening, salt, and pepper, the lowly yardbird was transformed into the finest after-church offertory, fit for the preacher himself if he stopped by. It was such a Sunday staple it was soon dubbed "the gospel bird."

Lots of food historians have tried to trace the dish's origins—typically followed by lots of shouting matches. Fried chicken is the multicultural progeny of many cooks—including the Scots, who fried chicken in fat while the English roasted and braised, as well as Vietnamese and even medieval Italian cooks, who served a version of it long before our country was discovered. African slaves added herbs and spices to the mix—and perhaps because many slaves were allowed to raise chickens, they perfected the dish in their own kitchens before it became a delicacy in plantation dining rooms. Like jazz and country music, fried chicken is an heirloom handed down from our hardscrabble and often painful past—perhaps only the hamburger rivals it for the most all-American dish.

As capital of the New South, Atlanta is the crossroads meeting-place for all Southerners' food habits. Here, we can all agree on one thing: no dish better represents our shared table.

That might be the last thing we all settle on because we've all got a different way of cooking it. Take Scott Peacock's method, developed with Edna Lewis: brined in buttermilk and fried in country ham-flavored lard. Or Lenn Storey's: always pan-fried in cast-iron skillets, like those once belonging to his father, Deacon Burton. Or the Ritz's Bennett Hollberg's recipe, twice-fried—once covered, and again uncovered in hotter oil.

Those are just a springboard for a few of fried chicken's close cousins: Dainty quail, from our plantations' heartland. Doro wot, the Ethiopian national dish, a spicy stew with whole hard-boiled eggs that might have served as a fried-chicken forerunner. Elegant Chinese duck, served with leeks. Smothered chicken, a relative of the European breaded, fried, and simmered fricassee. And a brand-new take on another old favorite, chicken and dumplings.

Southern Pan-Fried Chicken

WATERSHED, CHEF SCOTT PEACOCK

(FROM *THE GIFT OF SOUTHERN COOKING* BY
EDNA LEWIS AND SCOTT PEACOCK)

Serves 6 to 8 people

This labor-intensive recipe is the Tuesday night menu offering at Scott Peacock's restaurant, Watershed. Served with mashed potatoes and green beans, the plate is so popular it sometimes sells out by 7:30 pm.

1 (3-pound) chicken, cut into 8 pieces and brined for 8 to 12 hours

1 quart buttermilk

1 pound lard

$\frac{1}{2}$ cup unsalted butter

$\frac{1}{2}$ cup country ham pieces, or 1 thick slice country ham cut into
$\frac{1}{2}$-inch strips

1 cup flour

2 tablespoons cornstarch

1 teaspoon salt

$\frac{1}{2}$ teaspoon freshly ground black pepper

To prepare the chicken, drain the brined chicken and rinse out the bowl it was brined in. Return the chicken to the bowl and pour the buttermilk over it. Cover and refrigerate 8 to 12 hours. Drain the chicken on a wire rack, discarding the buttermilk.

Meanwhile, prepare the fat for frying by putting the lard, butter, and country ham into a heavy skillet or frying pan. Cook over low heat for 30 to 45 minutes, skimming as needed, until the butter ceases to throw off foam and the ham is browned. Using a slotted spoon, remove the ham carefully from the fat. (The ham pieces can be saved and used to make smoked pork stock.) Just before frying, increase the temperature to medium-high and heat the fat to 335 degrees F.

Prepare the dredge by blending flour, cornstarch, salt, and pepper in a shallow bowl or on wax paper.

Dredge the drained chicken pieces thoroughly in the flour mixture, then pat well to remove all excess flour.

Slip some of the chicken pieces, skin side down, into the heated fat, being careful not to overcrowd the pan. Fry in batches if necessary. Cook 8 to 10 minutes on each side, until the chicken is golden brown and cooked through. Drain thoroughly on a wire rack or on crumpled paper towels and serve.

Fried Chicken with Stone-Ground Grits and Collard Greens

THE ATLANTA GRILL, CHEF BENNETT HOLLBERG

Serves 10 to 12

Chef Bennett Hollberg's mother's recipe calls for my favorite, sweetest part of the bird: the legs.

Braised Greens

8 ounces applewood-smoked bacon, cut into $1/2$-inch pieces

1 sweet yellow onion, julienned

3 pounds collard greens, leaves chopped and stems discarded

$1/2$ cup apple cider vinegar

2 cups chicken stock, heated

Salt and freshly ground black pepper

Grits

$2\frac{1}{2}$ cups chicken stock

$2\frac{1}{2}$ cups milk

$2\frac{1}{2}$ cups cream

2 tablespoons salt, plus more to taste

1 teaspoon freshly ground black pepper, plus more to taste

2 cups stone-ground grits

$1/2$ cup sour cream

Fried Chicken

Vegetable oil, for deep-frying

$1/4$ cup curry powder

2 tablespoons ground black pepper

2 tablespoons paprika

2 tablespoons celery salt

2 tablespoons garlic salt

12 chicken drumsticks, skins removed

12 chicken thighs, skins removed

4 cups flour

To prepare the braised greens, slowly brown the bacon in a large pot over medium heat. When the bacon is crispy, add the onions and sauté until limp but not browned. Add the greens and stir. Add the vinegar and cook for about 5 minutes, until the greens are wilted. Add the stock. Season with salt and pepper and cook the greens for 45–60 minutes, stirring frequently, until the greens are tender but not too soft.

To prepare the grits, combine the chicken stock, milk, and cream in a saucepan and bring to a boil. Season with salt and pepper. Slowly

add the grits, whisking constantly. Reduce heat to a simmer and stir slowly and constantly for at least 2 minutes. Cook on low heat about 30 minutes, or until tender, stirring every 3–4 minutes to avoid clumping. Once all liquid has been absorbed and grits are soft, remove from heat and stir in sour cream. Adjust the seasoning and serve.

To make the fried chicken, in a large pot or deep skillet, heat the vegetable oil to 300–325 degrees F.

Combine the curry powder, pepper, paprika, celery salt, and garlic salt in a large bowl. Add the chicken and toss to coat and evenly distribute seasoning. In a separate bowl, dredge the chicken in the flour to lightly coat.

Add the chicken to the hot oil, cover the pot loosely with aluminum foil, and fry for about 15 minutes. Remove the chicken from the oil and allow to drain on wire racks. Meanwhile, increase the temperature of the oil to 375 degrees F.

Return the chicken to the hot oil and fry for about 5 minutes, or until dark golden brown. The meat of the chicken should be beginning to shrink away from the bone when it is fully cooked. Drain chicken on wire racks and serve immediately.

Cover the greens and grits to keep warm until served.

Fried Chicken

MARY MAC'S TEA ROOM, OWNER JOHN FERRELL

Serves 4

The city's meat-and-three standby makes its chicken probably pretty much like your mom did—if she'd run a beloved, prize-winning restaurant that to many defines old-school Atlanta dining.

Chicken

1 (3- to 3½-) pound fryer
   chicken, cut into 8 pieces

Salt and white pepper

Vegetable or peanut oil,
   for deep-frying

Coating

1 cup flour

1 teaspoon salt

½ teaspoon white pepper

Batter

1 cup tepid water

1 teaspoon salt

½ teaspoon white pepper

1 cup flour

Rinse the chicken under running water. Pat dry. Sprinkle with the salt and white pepper and set aside for 1 to 2 hours.

Fill a 12-inch frying pan or deep fryer half full of oil. Heat to 325 degrees F.

To make the batter, combine the water, salt, white pepper, and flour in a bowl and mix well. Place the chicken pieces in this batter.

To make the coating, combine the flour, salt, and white pepper. Lift the chicken from the batter and roll in the coating. Shake off any excess.

Fry for about 8 minutes on each side, until golden brown. Drain well on paper towels and serve.

Iron Skillet Fried Chicken

WISTERIA, CHEF JASON HILL

Serves 4

This updated-Southern restaurant serves a spicy one-pot meal, which includes chicken that is marinated and fried to perfection.

Chicken and Marinade

1 (2½- to 3-pound) chicken

2 cups buttermilk

1 tablespoon ancho
  chile powder

1 tablespoon paprika

¼ teaspoon ground
  cayenne pepper

Seasoned Flour

2 cups flour

2 tablespoons paprika

1 tablespoon salt

2 teaspoons ground
  white pepper

¼ teaspoon ground
  cayenne pepper

Cut the chicken into quarters and de-bone the leg and thigh.

Combine the buttermilk, chile powder, paprika, and cayenne pepper in a shallow dish. Add the chicken and turn to coat. Cover and refrigerate for at least 1 hour; marinating overnight is best.

To prepare the seasoned flour, combine the flour, paprika, salt, white pepper, and cayenne pepper in a bowl.

Fill an iron skillet with 1½ inches of vegetable oil and heat to 325 degrees F.

Lift the chicken out of the buttermilk and place directly into seasoned flour. Dredge in the flour, shake off any excess, and carefully slide into the hot oil. Fry 5–8 minutes, until golden brown outside and a thermometer stuck into the chicken reads 165 degrees F. Drain on paper towels.

Fried Chicken

SON'S PLACE, OWNER LENN STOREY

Serves 6

Lenn Storey and his family took over for his late father, Deacon Burton, who operated what was widely acknowledged as the best fried chicken emporium in town. No politician could miss a campaign stop at Deacon's without fear of losing an election. Lunchtime customers were treated to Burton's own midday pronouncements, preceded by the ringing of a little bell. At Son's Place, Storey faithfully fried his chicken in Deacon's big cast-iron skillets. Now Son's Place is gone too, but the recipe is handed down like a favorite stained index card from the family collection.

8 cups water

$\frac{1}{3}$ cup plus 1 teaspoon salt, divided

3 tablespoons plus $\frac{1}{2}$ teaspoon ground black pepper, divided

1 ($2\frac{1}{2}$-pound) chicken, cut into 6 pieces, leaving drumstick and thigh together

2 cups self-rising flour (White Lily brand is recommended)

Vegetable oil, for deep-frying

In a large mixing bowl, combine the water, $\frac{1}{3}$ cup salt, and 3 tablespoons pepper. Stir until the salt dissolves. Add the chicken to the brine, submerging all the pieces. Let soak 30 minutes.

Drain the chicken on a wire cooling rack placed over a rimmed baking sheet. Do not pat dry. Sprinkle with remaining 1 teaspoon salt and $\frac{1}{2}$ teaspoon pepper. Dredge the chicken pieces in the flour to coat.

Heat a large cast-iron skillet over medium heat. Add enough vegetable oil to come halfway up the sides of the pan. Heat the oil to 360 to 380 degrees F. Carefully add as many pieces of chicken as will fit in a single layer without crowding. Turn dark meat pieces after approximately 8 minutes and turn breasts after approximately 10 minutes. (Breasts take approximately 20 minutes to cook, wings 8 minutes, and drumstick/thighs 16 minutes).

Drain chicken on a clean cooling rack placed over a clean, rimmed baking sheet. Repeat until all the chicken is fried. Serve hot.

See photo on page 90.

Smothered Chicken

BUSY BEE CAFÉ, OWNER TRACY GATES

Serves 6 to 8

In Creole cooking, smothered dishes start with a dark, smoky roux. The Busy Bee's classic Southern version spices things up a bit but is more closely related to the European fricassee—a cut-up, dredged, fried, and then braised dish, here made with lighter chicken broth rather than cream.

5 cups water

1 tablespoon salt, plus more as needed

½ teaspoon Lawry's Seasoned Salt

½ teaspoon garlic powder

½ teaspoon black pepper, plus more as needed

1 (3½-pound) chicken, cut into 8 pieces

½ cup peanut oil

1 cup flour, divided

2 cups chopped onions

3 cups chicken broth

Combine the water, salt, seasoned salt, garlic powder, and pepper in a large plastic container and stir to blend. Add the chicken and marinate overnight in the refrigerator.

Remove the chicken from the marinade and drain.

Heat the oil in a large cast-iron skillet over medium-high heat. Dredge the chicken in ¾ cup flour and add to the skillet, in batches if necessary. Brown on all sides, about 12 minutes. Set the chicken aside and pour off the oil, reserving about 1 tablespoon.

Decrease the heat to medium-low and stir in the onions. Sauté for about 5 minutes, until tender. Gradually mix in the chicken broth and ¼ cup flour, stirring quickly to prevent lumps. If lumps form, add more water and continue to whip. Add salt and pepper to taste. Bring to a boil, stirring constantly, and then reduce the heat to low.

Return the chicken to the skillet, cover, and continue cooking for 30 minutes, until the chicken juices run clear and the gravy has thickened. Serve hot.

Balsamic Marinated Quail with Pine Nuts and Roasted Cauliflower

ECCO, CHEF MICAH WILLIX

Serves 6

Georgia's native bird gets a sweet and piquant touch with balsamic vinegar in this classic fall dish.

12 whole quail

½ cup balsamic vinegar

2 cups dark poultry stock or chicken stock

2 shallots, chopped

4 cloves garlic, minced

10 sprigs thyme

¼ cup olive oil

¼ cup butter, cut into small pieces

Salt and freshly ground black pepper

8 cups roasted cauliflower

¼ cup pine nuts, toasted

To marinate the quail, combine the quail, vinegar, stock, shallots, garlic, and thyme in a large bowl. Cover with plastic wrap and refrigerate for 12–24 hours.

Preheat a grill to medium. Remove the quail from the marinade. Pour the marinade into a small saucepan, add the oil, and bring to a simmer over medium heat. Cook until the liquid has reduced by three-quarters.

While the marinade is cooking, season the quail with salt and pepper. Grill the quail, uncovered, over a medium flame for about 15 minutes, until they are about medium done, or show just a little pink when cut open. Because of the sugar content of the marinade, the quail have a tendency to burn, so rotate often, watching carefully that they do not burn.

When the marinade is finished cooking, reduce the heat to low.

Slowly add the butter, one piece at a time, stirring to incorporate fully before adding the next piece. Strain the finished sauce and season to taste with salt and pepper.

Place the finished quail on a plate with the roasted cauliflower, drizzle with the sauce, and sprinkle the toasted pine nuts on top.

Chicken & Dumplings

CAKES & ALE, OWNERS BILLY AND KRISTIN ALLIN

Serves 8

This hip little Decatur haven for farm-to-table foodies offers a European-inspired twist to this Southern classic. The dumplings are actually the little potato-y dough puffs known in Italy as gnocchi.

Potato Dumplings

- 2 large russet or baking potatoes
- 1½ tablespoons salt
- 1 small egg or ½ large egg, lightly beaten
- 1 cup "00" flour (may substitute all-purpose flour)
- Rice flour, to dust
- 2 tablespoons butter

Chicken

- 1 (2½-pound) chicken
- 4 quarts chicken broth
- 1 large bay leaf
- 3 tablespoons butter, divided
- 1 carrot, diced
- 1 cup diced young turnip
- 1 rib celery, diced
- 1 onion, diced
- ¼ cup salt
- 2 tablespoons flour
- 1 cup fresh black-eyed peas
- 2 teaspoons vegetable oil
- ¼ pound wild mushrooms
- 1 teaspoon dried thyme
- ¼ cup heavy cream
- ¼ cup chopped fresh parsley
- 1½ teaspoons chopped fresh tarragon
- ½ teaspoon finely grated lemon zest
- Salt and freshly ground black pepper
- Freshly grated Parmesan cheese

To make the dumplings, cover the potatoes with water in a saucepan and boil until the potatoes are easily pierced with a knife, about 25 minutes. Remove from the water and let steam for 2 minutes. It is important to make the dough while the potatoes are still hot. Hold the hot potatoes in a towel with one hand and carefully remove the peels. Puree through a food mill or ricer onto a clean counter. Flatten the potato to make a circle about ½ inch thick. Sprinkle evenly with the salt and rub the egg over the surface. Evenly cover the surface of the potatoes with the 00 flour. Gently knead the dough until well combined and shape into a large log, 3 to 4 inches in diameter. Let rest 5 minutes.

To prepare the chicken, put the chicken into a large pot, cover with the broth, and add a bay leaf. Bring to a boil and skim off any impurities that rise to the surface. Turn off the heat, cover the pot, and leave the chicken for 1 hour.

Remove the chicken from the pot and strain the poaching liquid. (Reserve 4 cups for this recipe.) When the chicken is cool enough to handle, remove all chicken meat from the bones and set aside.

While the chicken is being poached, dust a sheet pan with rice flour.

Cut the dough into pieces 2 inches in length and roll each piece into a rope about 1/2 inch in diameter. Cut into dumplings approximately 1 inch long with a pastry cutter. Sprinkle with a little rice flour and gently toss to coat. Place on the prepared sheet pan.

Melt 2 tablespoons butter in a large saucepan and add the carrot, turnip, celery, onion, and salt. Sauté 3–5 minutes, until vegetables are limp. Add the flour and stir until vegetables are coated. Add the reserved poaching liquid and bring to a boil; skim fat from the surface. Simmer 15–20 minutes, until the liquid is thick.

To blanch the black-eyed peas, bring 2 quarts salted water to a rapid boil, add the peas, and cook until tender, about 20 minutes.

Heat a sauté pan to very hot and add the vegetable oil. Add the mushrooms and the remaining butter. Cook 5 minutes, until slightly brown.

Add the mushrooms, thyme, chicken, black-eyed peas, and cream to the simmering vegetable mixture. Heat through. Add the parsley, tarragon, lemon zest, and salt and pepper to taste. Keep warm.

Bring a large pot of water to a boil. Melt 2 tablespoons butter and pour into a bowl. Add the dumplings to the boiling water and cook only until they rise to the surface. Remove with a slotted spoon and put in the bowl with the butter. Toss to coat and sprinkle with salt.

Preheat the oven to 375 degrees F.

Pour the chicken mixture into 8 small or 1 large casserole dish. Cover chicken with dumplings and sprinkle with Parmesan cheese. Bake 10–15 minutes, until the top is slightly brown. Serve hot.

Duck with Beautiful Leeks

GRAND CHINA, OWNERS MR. K.C.
CHANG & MRS. TSE-CHIH CHANG

Serves 4

Husband-and-wife owners K. C. and Tse-Chih Chang are the gracious hosts at this Buckhead favorite, in business since 1978.

Marinade

- 1 teaspoon salt
- ½ teaspoon white pepper
- 1 teaspoon sugar
- 2 teaspoons soy sauce
- 1 tablespoon Chinese rice wine

Duck

- 1 (4- to 6-pound) whole duck
- 1 whole gingerroot, thinly sliced
- 5 scallions, trimmed
- 2 sprigs cilantro
- 12 whole leeks, trimmed
- 2 teaspoons ground cinnamon
- 2 teaspoons ground cumin
- 2 tablespoons oil

To make the marinade, combine the salt, white pepper, sugar, soy sauce, and rice wine in a large bowl. Clean the duck, removing any excess fat. Wash and pat dry. Using your hands, rub the skin of the duck with ginger, and do the same with the marinade, turning to coat evenly. Let the duck marinate for 20 minutes.

Place the duck in a greased pan and cover with a muslin cloth. Place the ginger slices, scallions, cilantro, leeks, cinnamon, and cumin on top of the muslin cloth. Place the pan in a steamer and steam for 1 to 1½ hours, until the duck is cooked through. Reserve the duck and leeks and discard the rest.

Heat oil to 250 degrees F in a large skillet. De-bone the steamed duck, slice into strips of equal size, about ¼ inch thick, and fry quickly in the oil.

Plate the sliced duck with the leeks and serve hot.

Duck Breast with Wild Rice and Walnuts, Duck Confit, Watercress, and Cranberries

PANO'S & PAUL'S, BUCKHEAD LIFE
RESTAURANT GROUP

4 servings

Duck Breast

- 2 whole ducks (remove breast and legs and reserve carcass)
- Kosher salt
- Black pepper
- 1 bunch watercress
- Lemon juice, to taste
- Olive oil, to taste

Wild Rice and Walnuts

- 3 cups chicken stock, divided
- Salt
- 1/2 cup wild rice
- 1/2 cup barley
- 1/2 cup orange juice
- 1/4 cup dried apricots
- 1/4 cup dried cranberries
- 2 shallots, minced
- 1/2 cup walnuts, toasted
- 2 tablespoons walnut oil
- 1 tablespoon chopped parsley

Duck Confit

- 4 duck legs
- Kosher salt
- 2 cloves garlic, chopped
- 2 bay leaves, crushed
- 2 sprigs thyme
- Duck fat, to cover

Duck Jus

- 2 duck carcasses, each cut into 4 pieces
- 2 cups large dice mirepoix
- 2 tablespoons honey
- 2 tablespoons maple syrup
- 2 cups orange juice
- 1/4 cup sherry vinegar
- 3 sprigs thyme
- 2 bay leaves
- 2 quarts chicken stock
- 4 quarts water

To cook the duck breast, trim the breast of excess fat and silver skin. Season the breasts with kosher salt and black pepper on both sides, then score each breast in a crisscross pattern. Place the breasts skin-side down in a large, cold sauté pan. Heat on low, allowing the skin to cook slowly to release its fat. The skin will become golden brown and crisp. Place flesh-side down in a 400 degrees F oven until desired doneness.

Remove the duck from pan and allow to rest.

For the Duck Confit, trim excess fat from legs and render. Place 2 legs in a pan flesh-side up. Cover with kosher salt, garlic, bay leaves, and thyme. Place remaining legs flesh-side down on top of seasoned legs. Cover with plates to press, use plastic wrap to cover, and refrigerate overnight.

Remove legs and place in a clean baking pan. Cover with hot duck fat and parchment paper, and cover the pan with foil. Bake in a 350-degree oven for 3–4 hours. Check for doneness. The bones should pull away from meat when done. Cool and store in duck fat.

Season 1½ cups stock with salt and bring to a simmer. Add wild rice and cook 30–45 minutes, until tender but not mushy.

About 20 minutes after rice starts cooking, bring the remaining stock to a simmer in a separate pot. Add the barley and cook for 45 minutes.

While rice and barley are cooking, heat orange juice to a simmer. Add apricots and cranberries. Remove from heat and let bloom. Drain.

Remove skin and bones from duck confit. Shred meat.

Heat sauté pan over medium heat. Add shallots and cook for 2 minutes, until soft. Add remaining duck confit and Wild Rice and Walnuts ingredients. Season to taste and stir until well mixed.

For the Duck Jus, roast duck bones in a 400-degree oven for 30 minutes until lightly browned. Remove fat from pan and add mirepoix. Roast for 15 minutes. Add honey and maple syrup. Stir well and roast until nicely caramelized.

While bones are roasting, bring orange juice and sherry vinegar to a boil. Reduce to simmer and cook until reduced by two-thirds.

Add bones and citrus reduction to stockpot, along with the thyme and bay leaves. Cover with stock and water. Bring to a boil and reduce heat to a simmer. Skim excess fat from surface throughout cooking. Cook for 1½ hours and strain. Discard bones and vegetables.

Return stock to sauce pan and simmer. Reduce to sauce consistency.

To plate, slice duck breast thinly on a bias and place on the wild rice salad. Dress watercress with a light coating of lemon juice and olive oil, and place next to breast. Spoon the duck jus around.

Doro Wot

Serves 6

At Queen of Sheba, diners enjoy this classic Ethiopian chicken stew in the traditional way: by soaking it up with injera, the pleasantly spongy and malty national bread.

2 pounds chicken legs and thighs, skinless

Juice of 1 lemon

2 teaspoons salt

2 onions, chopped

3 cloves garlic, crushed

1 tablespoon peeled and chopped fresh ginger

¼ cup oil or unsalted butter

2 tablespoons paprika

¼ cup berbere paste (available online)

¾ cup water or chicken stock

¼ cup red wine

1 teaspoon cayenne pepper

Cardamom, to taste

Salt and freshly ground black pepper

6 hard-boiled eggs, shelled

Mix together the chicken, lemon juice, and salt in a large bowl and set aside to marinate for about 30 minutes.

While the chicken is marinating, combine the onions, garlic, and ginger in a food processor or blender and puree, adding a little water if necessary to make a smooth paste.

Heat the oil in a large saucepan over medium heat. Stir in the paprika to color the oil and cook for about 1 minute; do not let the mixture burn. Stir in the berbere paste and cook for another 2 to 3 minutes.

Add the onion-garlic-ginger puree and sauté until most of the moisture evaporates and the onion cooks down and loses its raw aroma, 5 to 10 minutes; do not allow the mixture to burn.

Pour in the water and wine and stir in the chicken pieces and cayenne. Season with cardamom, salt, and pepper. Bring to a boil, reduce heat to low, cover, and simmer for 45 minutes. Add water as necessary to maintain a saucy consistency. Add the whole hard-boiled eggs and continue to cook for another 10–15 minutes, until the chicken is cooked through and very tender.

Adjust the seasoning and serve hot with injera bread or rice.

Classic Bistro Skirt Steak and Frites
French American Brasserie

Meats
Hooves & Trotters

Some credit air-conditioning with making Atlanta a business powerhouse. Lord knows we could never live without it now—the days when sweltering, oppressive heat went on for weeks without a respite are blessedly past. But we lost a few things along with those days, like eating outside in the cool of the evening. And when you did finally have supper (never "dinner"), it was more likely to be something lighter—chicken or fish, maybe followed by some hand-cranked ice cream. Heavier meats, like beef, pork, lamb, and venison, were fall dishes, when hunting and slaughtering season coincided with the onset of weather that made these substantial dishes welcome fuel for your personal pot-bellied stove.

Along with wintry, braised dishes, in this chapter you'll find the city's best—and most fun—hamburgers and hot dogs, those perennial hot-weather beach and poolside favorites. These heavyweights would be sure to trigger Mom's warning to wait at least an hour before swimming to avoid "cramps." An hour after eating the bust-a-gut Vandross burger, though, you're far more likely to be power-napping than body-surfing.

Beef and Mushroom Tarts

PARK 75 AT THE FOUR SEASONS,
CHEF ROBERT GERSTENECKER

Serves 4

The Four Seasons' elegant dining room serves the most tender cut of beef with a classic mushroom tart.

2 to 3 tablespoons blended oil

12 cups trimmed beef cheeks

1 carrot, diced

1 onion, diced

1 rib celery, diced

5 cloves garlic

3 tablespoons tomato paste

3 bay leaves

2 sprigs rosemary

1 cup red wine

8 cups unsalted beef broth

Mushroom Tart

3 (9½ x 9¼-inch) sheets puff pastry, defrosted if frozen

1 large egg, lightly beaten

1 leek, trimmed and diced

2 teaspoons butter

1 cup heavy cream

1½ tablespoons olive oil

3 cups chanterelle mushrooms, cleaned

2 cups fava beans, pod and skin removed, then blanched

Salt and ground black pepper

1 tomato, seeded and diced

1 tablespoon chopped fresh parsley

1 bunch baby greens

1 truffle, for garnish (optional)

Heat the oil in a large heavy-bottom saucepan over medium-high heat. Add the beef cheeks and sauté each side for 2 minutes on high heat until golden. Remove from pan. Add the carrot, onion, celery, and garlic; sauté until browned, about 5 minutes. Add the tomato paste, bay leaves, rosemary, and wine; bring to a boil. Reduce by half. Return beef cheeks to the pan with the beef broth. Bring to a boil, reduce to a simmer, cover, and cook 1–1½ hours, until beef is tender.

Remove beef from the pan and keep warm. Strain the braising liquid, return to the pan, and boil to reduce by half. Return the beef cheeks to the reduced braising liquid and let rest for 30 minutes.

Preheat the oven to 400 degrees F.

Using a 3-inch-round cutter, cut out eight 3-inch circles of puff pastry. Place 4 of the circles on a baking sheet and brush with beaten egg. Use a 2-inch-round cutter to cut circles in the remaining 4 pieces of puff pastry. Remove the center to form rings. Place rings on top of the pastry on the baking sheet. Brush with the egg wash. With a fork, prick the center of the shells, but not the rings. Refrigerate 30 minutes.

Bake 10 minutes, until beginning to brown. Reduce heat to 350 degrees F; bake 15 to 20 minutes more, until golden. Cool on a wire rack.

Combine the leek in a pan with the butter over medium heat, cover, and sweat until soft, about 10 minutes. Add the cream and cook until the cream is reduced by half.

Heat the oil in a large skillet over medium-high heat. Add the mushrooms and sauté until the moisture has seeped out. In a separate pot, cook the fava beans for 3–5 minutes, until tender, and add the leeks. Then add the fava beans and the leeks to the skillet mixture. Season to taste with salt and pepper. Stir in the tomato and parsley. Spoon into the tart shells.

Taste the beef cheeks and adjust seasoning. Top shells with beef cheeks. Garnish with greens and truffle.

Beef Brisket

BAGEL PALACE, OWNERS MANNY
KLEIN AND JOE WEINER

Serves 10

*Bagel Palace's classic Jewish holiday centerpiece is made the way Miss Daisy
probably prepared it: with ketchup, onion soup mix, and Coca-Cola.*

1 teaspoon Jane's Krazy Mixed-Up Salt

1 (5- to 6-pound) brisket

1/2 cup vegetable oil

2 carrots, thinly sliced

1 small white onion, chopped

1 packet onion soup mix

1 tablespoon onion powder

1 tablespoon garlic powder

1 teaspoon freshly ground black pepper

1 cup Coca-Cola

1 cup ketchup

Preheat the oven to 375 degrees F.

Rub the salt into the brisket. Heat the oil in a large skillet over
medium-high heat. Add the meat and brown on both sides. Transfer
to a 9 x 13-inch pan.

Mix together the carrots, onion, soup mix, onion powder, garlic
powder, black pepper, Coca-Cola, and ketchup. Pour over the brisket.

Cover with aluminum foil and roast 4 hours, until the meat is
fork-tender.

When the brisket is cooled, slice against the grain and serve.

Braised Country-Style Pork Ribs with Saffron Risotto

THE BLUE BICYCLE,
OWNERS GUY AND KATI OWEN

Serves 6

Dawsonville is at the outer limits of what most would consider Atlanta's satellite villages, but this little French bistro in a strip mall near Dawsonville's sprawling Premium Outlet Mall serves up classic Gallic dishes with a Southern twist, along with wines from North Georgia.

$\frac{1}{2}$ cup peanut oil, for frying

4 to 5 pounds thick-cut country-style pork ribs (6 to 8 pieces), trimmed of excess fat

Salt and white pepper

$\frac{1}{2}$ cup flour, for dredging

1 yellow onion, finely diced

1 carrot, finely diced

1 rib celery, finely diced

2 to 3 cloves garlic, minced

$\frac{1}{4}$ teaspoon dried red pepper flakes, or more to taste

$\frac{1}{2}$ cup dry white wine

1 (28-ounce) can Italian-style tomatoes

Zest of $\frac{1}{2}$ lemon, finely grated, plus finely grated zest for garnish

3 cups chicken stock

4 sprigs fresh thyme or $\frac{1}{2}$ teaspoon dried

8 large fresh sage leaves or $\frac{1}{2}$ teaspoon dried

1 bay leaf

Saffron Risotto (recipe follows)

Chopped fresh parsley

Preheat the oven to 325 degrees F.

Heat the oil in a 10-inch frying pan over medium-high heat to 350 degrees F on a frying thermometer. Season the ribs with salt and white pepper and dust them lightly with flour. Gently slide half the ribs into the oil. Do not crowd the pan; you can do them in two or three batches, if necessary. Brown 5 to 8 minutes on one side, then 4 to 5 minutes on the second side, and then remove them to a separate ovenproof pan or casserole large enough to hold all the ribs plus the liquid. You could use a turkey roaster for this.

Once all the ribs have been browned, reduce the heat to medium and pour off all but about 2 tablespoons of the oil. Add the onion, carrot, and celery and sauté the vegetables for about 10 minutes, stirring occasionally, until they are golden brown; scrape loose any brown bits that may have stuck to the pan from the ribs. Add the garlic and red pepper and cook for another minute.

Add the wine and bring it to a boil. Reduce the wine to half its original volume. Add the tomatoes, lemon zest, chicken stock, thyme, and sage. Taste the sauce and add salt and black pepper to taste. Remember that the sauce will reduce some during cooking and will intensify the flavor as it reduces. You can add more salt and pepper at the end, so don't overseason at this point. Add the bay leaf, return the sauce to a full boil, and then carefully pour it over the ribs. There should be enough sauce to come about halfway up the sides of the meat; it should not cover it completely. Cover the pan with a tight-fitting lid or aluminum foil and bake for 2 hours.

Remove the ribs from the oven and check for tenderness. They should be falling from the bone at this point. Allow to cool for 20 minutes while you begin the risotto recipe.

Carefully skim as much of the excess oil and fat from the top of the sauce as you can. Discard the fat. If the sauce seems thin, transfer the ribs to another dish and pour the sauce into a large saucepan. Cook over medium heat until it has reduced and thickened to your liking. Taste and adjust the salt and pepper, if needed.

To serve, divide the risotto among six large pasta bowls and top with one or two ribs each. Ladle on the sauce and sprinkle with plenty of parsley. Additional zest at this time is also a wonderful complement.

continued on page 121

Saffron Risotto

Serves 6

½ teaspoon saffron threads

½ cup dry white wine

6 to 8 cups chicken stock or water

1 tablespoon olive oil

2 tablespoons unsalted butter, divided

¼ cup finely chopped yellow onion

1½ cups Arborio or carnaroli rice, rinsed in cold water

Salt and white pepper (about 1½ teaspoons each)

2 ounces Parmesan cheese, freshly grated

Combine the saffron and the wine in a microwave-proof dish and microwave on high for 30 seconds. Let stand 15 minutes to infuse.

Heat the stock to a boil in a large saucepan; reduce to simmering.

Heat the olive oil and 1 tablespoon butter in a large saucepan over medium-high heat. Add the onion, reduce the heat, and sauté gently for 3 to 5 minutes until translucent, being careful not to brown. Add the rice and sauté about 2 minutes, stirring occasionally, until warmed through. Carefully add the wine and the saffron threads. Don't get burned by the steam! Stir until the wine has been absorbed by the rice. Add about 1 cup of the simmering stock to the rice. Keep the burner set to a medium-high heat; you want to gently boil, not simmer. Stir once or twice. Watch the pot carefully, stirring occasionally but not constantly. Add some salt and white pepper at this point. Once the stock has been absorbed, add another cup of stock and stir as before. Repeat until the rice has absorbed enough stock to become al dente with a creamy sauce-like coating. It should not be hard in the center, but it should not be so tender as to be mushy, either. There is no exact amount of stock, it might take all of 6 cups, or it may not. Experience is the best guide.

Once the rice is cooked to al dente, remove the pan from the heat and stir in the Parmesan cheese and the remaining 1 tablespoon butter. Adjust the salt and pepper to taste and serve at once.

Braised Lamb "Lasagna"

4TH & SWIFT, CHEF JAY SWIFT

Serves 8 to 10

Known for his deft small plates that reinvent the food wheel, Jay Swift serves a deconstructed "lasagna" with tender braised lamb in his Fourth Street Ward restaurant

Lamb Braise

- 3 tablespoons vegetable oil
- 1 (2- to 4-pound) lamb shoulder roast, boned, rolled, and tied
- 3 carrots, cubed
- 2 Vidalia onions, cubed
- 1 bunch celery, cubed
- 4 cloves garlic, crushed
- 1/2 cup tomato paste
- 3/4 cup red wine
- 3 cups demi-glace
- 3 cups chicken stock
- 1 sprig rosemary
- 5 sprigs thyme
- 1 bunch parsley
- 1 bay leaf
- 6 peppercorns

Pasta

- 3 1/2 cups "00" pasta flour, or all-purpose flour
- 1/2 teaspoon salt
- 4 large eggs
- 1 tablespoon extra virgin olive oil

To finish

- 1/2 cup ricotta cheese
- Juice of 1 lemon
- 1 teaspoon chopped fresh thyme
- 1 teaspoon chopped fresh rosemary
- 1 teaspoon chopped fresh sage
- 1 tablespoon extra virgin olive oil
- 1 cup julienned fresh shiitake mushrooms
- 1 tablespoon butter
- 1 teaspoon minced garlic
- 1 teaspoon diced shallots
- 1/2 cup brunois mirepoix (equal parts celery, carrots, and onions), chopped
- 1 tomato, peeled and diced
- Salt and freshly ground black pepper
- Parmesan cheese, for shaving

Preheat the oven to 300 degrees F.

To prepare the lamb braise, in a large Dutch oven, heat the oil over medium-high heat. Add the lamb and sear on all sides until golden. Remove and set aside. Decrease heat to medium and add carrots, onions, celery, and garlic. Sauté, stirring frequently, until the vegetables begin to brown. Add the tomato paste and cook, stirring frequently to prevent burning, 2 minutes. Add the wine and boil until the liquid is reduced by half. Add the remaining ingredients. Bring to a simmer. Return the lamb to the pan. Cover and put in the oven to braise for about 2 hours, until the lamb is tender.

Remove the meat from the pan and set aside until cool to the touch. Pick the lamb into large chunks. Set aside.

Strain the braising liquid through a chinois or other strainer into a large pot to remove the herbs and vegetables. Bring the liquid to a simmer, skimming frequently with a ladle to remove excess fat. Reduce until the liquid has a saucy consistency.

To make the pasta, combine the flour and salt in a mixing bowl. Add the eggs and stir until the mixture comes together, adding the oil at the end of the mixing process.

Turn the dough out onto a lightly floured surface and knead for 5 minutes, until a smooth dough forms. Wrap in plastic wrap and refrigerate 1 hour. Roll the pasta through pasta maker until you have a thin sheet. Cut into 2-inch squares.

To finish the dish, mix the ricotta with the lemon juice, thyme, rosemary, and sage. Set aside.

Heat the olive oil in a sauté pan over medium-high heat. Add mushrooms and sauté until they begin to wilt, about 3 minutes. Add the butter. When the butter is melted, add the garlic, shallots, and mirepoix. When the mirepoix is translucent, add the tomato and 2 cups reserved braising liquid. Bring to a simmer, then add 2 cups lamb chunks. When thoroughly hot, season to taste.

Cook the pasta in boiling salted water until al dente. Place on towels to drain.

Preheat the oven to 400 degrees F.

To serve, place a spoonful of braised lamb on an ovenproof plate, then a spoonful of ricotta. Place pasta over and repeat. Finish with a ricotta on top. Bake for 4 minutes. Top with Parmesan and serve.

Grilled Lamb Tenderloin

COM VIETNAMESE, OWNER DUC TRAN

Serves 4

One of Buford Highway's best Vietnamese restaurants, Com specializes in grilled dishes like this delectable lamb tenderloin.

1 (2- to 2½-pound) lamb tenderloin or boneless
    leg of lamb, thinly sliced

6 cloves garlic, minced

2 teaspoons minced fresh ginger

4 teaspoons Vietnamese fish sauce

3 tablespoons plus 1 teaspoon sugar

1 tablespoon honey

1 teaspoon curry powder

4 teaspoons Chinese five-spice powder

1 tablespoon rice wine

1 teaspoon oyster sauce

1 teaspoon soy sauce

2 teaspoons Asian sesame oil

Combine the lamb with the garlic, ginger, fish sauce, sugar, honey, curry powder, five-spice powder, rice wine, oyster sauce, soy sauce, and sesame oil. Marinate in the refrigerator for 24 hours, turning occasionally.

Grill at medium-high heat, 250 degrees F, for about 4 minutes, or until slightly brown.

Classic Bistro Skirt Steak and Frites

FRENCH AMERICAN BRASSERIE,
CHEF STEVE SHARP

Serves 6

"Bistro" means fast—as in, the time it takes to make this traditional French steak.

Soy Vinaigrette Marinade

- 1 large shallot
- 2 cloves garlic
- 1/2 cup soy sauce
- 1/4 cup aged Spanish sherry vinegar
- 1 tablespoon cold water, plus more as needed
- Juice of 1 lime
- Black pepper
- 1 1/2 cups grapeseed oil

Steak

- 3 pounds skirt steak, cut into 8-ounce portions

Bistro Butter

- 1 pound salted butter, at room temperature
- 1 bunch parsley, finely chopped
- 10 cloves garlic, chopped
- 3 large shallots, finely chopped

Frites

- 4 large Idaho or russet potatoes, unpeeled, sliced into 1/4-inch-thick sticks
- Vegetable oil, for frying
- Salt and freshly ground black pepper
- 1 pound watercress, tough stems discarded

To make the soy vinaigrette, combine the shallot, garlic, soy sauce, vinegar, water, and lime juice in a blender. Season lightly with black pepper. Blend on low for 10 seconds. Increase the blending speed to medium and slowly add the oil to form an emulsion. Continue to add the oil to a desired consistency. If the marinade is too thick, blend in additional water. Season with salt and pepper to taste.

Place the skirt steak in a shallow baking dish; add about half of the soy vinaigrette and turn to coat the meat. Set the remaining vinaigrette aside.

To make the flavored butter, combine the butter, parsley, garlic, and shallots. Fold together until the mixture is smooth. Set aside in the refrigerator.

Blanch the potatoes in boiling water for 10 minutes and shock in ice water to stop the cooking. Drain well.

Preheat a grill or broiler to high.

Heat enough vegetable oil to cover the potatoes in a heavy saucepan or deep-fryer to 350 degrees F.

Remove the meat from the marinade and season with black pepper. Grill or broil 3–5 minutes on each side, depending on its thickness, to achieve medium doneness. Let rest for 10 minutes to allow the juices to settle.

While the steak is resting, pat the potatoes well to ensure they are dry. Drop the potatoes into the hot oil and fry for 5 minutes, or until golden brown. Season with salt and pepper and melted bistro butter. Toss until well coated.

Toss the watercress with the remaining vinaigrette and top the steak with more of the bistro butter. Plate and serve.

Vandross Burger

GRAVITY PUB, OWNERS JOSH
AND ALLIE WESTBERRY

Serves 4

Thought you'd had it all? How about this gilded-lily version of the classic American burger served Southern-style: with cheese and applewood-smoked bacon on a Krispy Kreme doughnut "bun."

1 pound ground beef

1 teaspoon black pepper

1 teaspoon kosher salt

½ teaspoon garlic powder

4 slices cheddar cheese

12 slices applewood-smoked bacon, cooked

4 glazed doughnuts (Krispy Kreme is recommended)

Preheat a grill to medium-high heat.

Mix together the beef, black pepper, salt, and garlic powder. Form into four burger patties.

Grill the burgers to the desired stage of doneness, 3–5 minutes per side, adding the cheese slice at the end of the cooking and letting it melt on the burger.

Top each burger with three bacon slices.

Slice each doughnut and toast the halves. Place the burgers between the toasted doughnuts, with the sugar-glazed side facing the meat. Serve immediately.

Country Fried Steak

HORSERADISH GRILL, CHEF DANIEL ALTERMAN

Serves 8

A perfect example of how putting a little energy into even an inexpensive cut of meat can turn it into something great. Dredged, fried, and then simmered with gravy, the perfect country-fried steak is meaty but fork-tender.

Gravy

2 cups chicken stock

¼ cup butter

2 cups heavy cream

½ teaspoon black pepper

Steak

8 (6-ounce) cube steaks

1 cup buttermilk

Vegetable oil, for deep-frying

Seasoned flour

1½ cups flour (White Lily brand is recommended)

¼ cup cornstarch

1 tablespoon garlic powder

1 tablespoon onion powder

1 tablespoon finely ground sea salt

1 tablespoon white pepper

¼ cup potato starch

To prepare the gravy, bring the chicken stock to a boil. Add the butter, cream, and pepper; boil to reduce slightly. Immediately cool in an ice bath. Gravy can be reheated for serving hot.

To prepare the seasoned flour, combine the flour, cornstarch, garlic powder, onion powder, salt, white pepper, and potato starch in a bowl and mix well.

To prepare the steak, use a meat tenderizer to flatten and tenderize the meat. Dip in the buttermilk, then coat with the seasoned flour mixture.

Heat 4 inches of oil in a large skillet or deep-fryer to 350 degrees F. Add the meat and fry for 3 minutes. Drain and pat dry with paper towels.

To serve, ladle 3 tablespoons of the heated gravy over the steak and serve.

Chef Gary's "39 Hour" Short Ribs

PANO'S & PAUL'S, BUCKHEAD LIFE
RESTAURANT GROUP

Serves 4

The price point is far lower than caviar or foie gras, but few foods match the luxurious taste and texture of slow-cooked short ribs. Clocking in with a cooking time of 39 hours, these ribs melt into velvet slices, scented with garlic, red wine, and shallots.

Veal Sauce

- 1 teaspoon plus 1 tablespoon vegetable oil, divided
- 1/2 cup mushrooms, sliced
- 1 tablespoon chopped shallots
- 1 teaspoon minced garlic
- 1 cup red wine
- 6 sprigs thyme
- 2 bay leaves
- 4 cups veal or beef stock

- 2 (2-pound) whole slabs boneless short ribs
- Kosher salt and freshly cracked black pepper

Garnish

- 8 slices bacon
- 20 baby carrots
- 12 button mushrooms
- 8 cipollini
- 4 teaspoons chives
- 1 pound Tagliatelle pasta, or fettuccini
- 2 tablespoons butter
- 2 tablespoons Parmesan cheese
- Parsley, to taste

Heat 1 teaspoon oil in a large saucepan over low heat. Add the mushrooms, shallots, and garlic. Cover and sweat until softened, about 5 minutes.

Add the wine, thyme, and bay leaves; bring to a boil over medium-high heat. Cook until the wine is reduced in volume by two-thirds. Add the veal stock and reduce by half. Strain and reserve.

Trim the ribs of any fat and silver skin. Cut each rib into 3 x 4-inch pieces (2 pieces per rib), and season with salt and black pepper.

Heat the remaining oil in a large skillet over high heat and sear the short ribs until nicely colored on both sides.

Place the ribs in cooking bags with the reduced veal sauce. Seal with a vacuum sealer.

Cook over an induction burner for 39 hours at 148 degrees F. Alternatively, place the seared short ribs and sauce in a braising pan or Dutch oven, cover with the lid, and braise in a 150-degree oven for 39 hours.

For the garnish, chop bacon into $\frac{1}{4}$-inch julienne strips. On medium heat, sauté bacon for 2 to 4 minutes until lightly brown. Add baby carrots, mushrooms, cipollini, and chives. Sauté 15 to 20 minutes, until cipollini are translucent.

Cook the pasta until tender. Toss with butter, Parmesan cheese, and parsley, and set aside until plating.

Spread cooked pasta on a plate, place short ribs (sliced, as an option) on center of pasta and top with vegetable garnish. Spoon sauce around the ribs and on top of the pasta, and serve.

"Shaking" Filet Mignon

NAM, OWNERS CHRIS AND ALEX KINJO

Serves 2

In a typical stir-fry, thin beef slices are rapidly tossed around a hot wok, but this traditional Vietnamese dish calls for whole cubes of steak (in this case, filet mignon) to be "shaken" with its soy-oyster sauce marinade.

2 teaspoons sugar
1 tablespoon oyster sauce
1 teaspoon Kimlan soy paste (available online)
1 clove garlic, diced
Pinch of black pepper
6 ounces beef tenderloin, cubed
Canola oil

Melt the sugar in a small frying pan over medium heat, taking care not to burn it. Transfer to a shallow bowl and add the oyster sauce, soy paste, garlic, and pepper. Stir to thoroughly blend. Add the steak cubes and marinate about 5 minutes.

Heat a large iron wok over high heat. Pour in enough oil to coat the entire wok. Immediately add the beef along with the marinade and stir-fry until cooked to your desire (rare, medium, or well). Serve immediately over stir-fried vegetables.

Grilled Pork Chops with Mustard Compote and Roasted Sweet Potatoes

WAHOO!, CHEF SCOTT WARREN

Serves 4

The little Decatur restaurant by the railroad tracks has a rich inner life—and one of the most pleasant patios in town. Neighbors have wholeheartedly embraced it for its smart, Southern cooking, judicious prices and well-mixed cocktails.

Mustard Compote

¼ cup unsalted butter

4 shallots, diced

1 cup Dijon mustard

½ cup ketchup

2 cups heavy cream

½ cup brown sugar

2 teaspoons celery seeds

1 teaspoon salt

½ teaspoon freshly ground
   black pepper

Roasted Sweet Potatoes

4 pounds sweet potatoes,
   peeled and diced

1 cup unsalted butter, melted

2 teaspoons ground cinnamon

½ cup maple syrup

½ cup brown sugar

½ teaspoon salt

½ teaspoon freshly ground
   black pepper

Pork Chops

8 (4-ounce) pork chops, bone in

2 tablespoons olive oil

Cracked black pepper

Start a charcoal or wood fire or preheat a gas grill to medium-high. Meanwhile, prepare the compote.

To make the compote, melt the butter in a saucepan over medium heat. Add the shallots and sauté until translucent, 3 to 5 minutes. Add the mustard, ketchup, cream, brown sugar, celery seeds, salt, and ground pepper and stir well. Heat long enough to dissolve the brown sugar. Set aside to cool.

To prepare the pork chops, rub the chops with olive oil and

sprinkle with cracked pepper. Sear the chops over the hottest part of the fire for a minute or two per side, taking care not to burn them. Move to a cooler spot on the grill and cook, turning once or twice until done, 10 to 20 minutes, depending on the thickness of the chops and whether you cover the grill. Pink inside is perfect.

Preheat the oven to 400 degrees F.

Combine the sweet potatoes, butter, cinnamon, maple syrup, brown sugar, salt, and pepper in a nonreactive bowl. Transfer to a nonstick baking pan or casserole dish. Cover and bake for 30 minutes.

Remove the cover and continue to bake for another 20 to 30 minutes, until the sweet potatoes are golden brown around the edges and soft through the inside. Serve hot.

Berkshire Pork Schnitzel with Grilled Vidalia Onion Salad, Parsley, and Peanuts

SHAUN'S EDGEWOOD SOCIAL CLUB,
CHEF/OWNER SHAUN DOTY

Serves 4

Chef Shaun Doty has a genius for translating new American dishes for a Southern accent. This classic German dish incorporates two of our best native ingredients: peanuts and Vidalia onions, with prized pork from the famed Berkshire "black pig."

Vidalia Onion Salad

- 2 Vidalia onions, sliced into 1/4-inch rings
- 1 teaspoon extra virgin olive oil
- 1 teaspoon roasted peanut oil
- 1/4 cup dry-roasted peanuts
- 1/4 cup fresh flat-leaf parsley leaves
- 1/2 cup shaved Parmigiano-Reggiano
- Salt and freshly ground black pepper

Pork Schnitzel

- 3 eggs
- 1/2 cup water
- 4 (5-ounce) portions Berkshire pork loin, pounded to scallopini thickness
- Salt and freshly ground black pepper
- 1 cup flour
- 2 cups panko (Japanese bread crumbs)
- 2 to 4 tablespoons vegetable oil
- 2 lemons, sliced into wedges

Preheat a grill to high heat.

To prepare the onion salad, skewer the onion rings and blanch in boiling salted water for 3 minutes. Drain well. Brush the onions with the olive oil and place on the hot grill. Grill the onions for 2 to 3 minutes, until lightly charred but still somewhat crisp. Transfer to a bowl and add the peanut oil, peanuts, parsley, and Parmigiano-Reggiano. Season with salt and pepper and toss to combine. Set aside.

Combine 3 eggs and water and whisk together to create an egg wash.

To prepare the pork, season both sides of each slice with salt and pepper. Dust with flour, coat with the egg wash, and dredge through the panko until thoroughly coated.

Heat a large sauté pan over medium-high heat. Add 2 tablespoons or more vegetable oil and place the pork comfortably in the pan without crowding. Fry until well browned on both sides, 4 to 6 minutes total cooking time. Keep warm while you continue to cook the remaining pork.

To serve, divide the pork among four pre-warmed plates. Spoon the onion salad over the pork. Garnish with lemon wedges and serve immediately.

Sweet Onion Slaw Dogs

BARKER'S RED HOTS, OWNER GLENN ROBINS

Serves 8

Serve over charcoal-broiled hot dogs straight off the grill!

1 cup sugar

1 teaspoon salt

1 teaspoon dry mustard powder

1 teaspoon celery seed

1 Vidalia or other sweet onion, grated

2 tablespoons vegetable oil

½ cup distilled white vinegar

1 head green cabbage, shredded

Combine the sugar, salt, mustard powder, and celery seed in a saucepan. Add the sweet onion, oil, and vinegar. Heat until the sugar is melted. Cool and refrigerate 1 hour.

Mix the dressing with the cabbage. Let rest for several hours, stir, and serve.

Pulled Pork BBQ on Cornmeal Pancakes with Spicy Mustard Coleslaw

HORSERADISH GRILL, CHEF DANIEL ALTERMAN

Serves 8

How to consolidate the barbecue platter experience: ditch the bun and the stale chips, keep the cornbread and the slaw. No, wait: use the cornbread as the bun . . . No, no, wait, I've got it: ditch the plate, and pile the barbecue on a flat cornmeal pancake, topped with slaw! Perfect!

Dry rub

    2 tablespoons chili powder

    2 tablespoons paprika

    1/3 teaspoon dry mustard

    1/3 teaspoon sage

    1/3 teaspoon cumin

For BBQ

    2 cups Worcestershire sauce

    1/2 cup dry rub

    1 (8- to 10-pound) pork
        butt, tenderized

Tomato BBQ Sauce

    1/2 pound bacon, sliced
        1/4 inch thick

    3/4 cup yellow onions, julienned

    1/3 cup apple cider vinegar

    4 tablespoons dark brown sugar

    1/4 tablespoon yellow mustard

    3 1/2 cups chili sauce

    1 3/4 cups ketchup

    1 teaspoon cup minced garlic

    1 teaspoon black pepper

    1 teaspoon molasses

    1 dash Tabasco Sauce

BBQ Marinade

    2 cups apple cider vinegar

    1 cup white vinegar

    1 teaspoon crushed red
        pepper flakes

    1 teaspoon cayenne pepper

    1 teaspoon black pepper

    2 teaspoons salt

    1 dash dry mustard powder

Spicy Mustard Slaw

    1 cup mayonnaise

    1 cup apple cider vinegar

    1 cup sugar

    1 1/4 teaspoons dry
        mustard powder

    4 cups shredded cabbage

continued on page 144

Cornmeal Scallion Pancake

1⅛ cups yellow cornmeal

⅔ cup flour

1 teaspoon baking soda

½ tablespoon salt

1 large egg

¾ cup buttermilk

1 tablespoon finely
  chopped scallions

2 tablespoons lard, melted

1 cup butter

To make the dry rub, combine all ingredients in a bowl. Coat the pork with the Worcestershire sauce and dredge it in the dry rub, rubbing it into all sides of the meat. Marinate in the refrigerator for 12 hours. Smoke at 325 degrees F for 8 hours.

Meanwhile, make the BBQ sauce. Brown the bacon in a large saucepan over medium heat. Add the onions and sauté until softened, about 3 minutes. Stir in the remaining ingredients. Simmer 1 hour, stirring often. Strain well and chill. Serve at room temperature.

To make the BBQ marinade, combine all ingredients in a medium saucepan. Set aside.

To make the slaw, whisk together the mayonnaise, cider vinegar, sugar, and mustard powder. Add the dressing to the cabbage and mix well.

Discard the outer skin of the pork and pull the meat into shreds. Add the pork to the marinade in the saucepan and heat over low heat while you make the pancakes.

To make the pancakes, whisk together the cornmeal, flour, baking soda, salt, egg, buttermilk, and scallions. Heat the lard and whisk into the batter. For each pancake, melt 2 teaspoons butter in a large frying pan over medium-high heat. Ladle 6 tablespoons of batter into a frying pan and cook on both sides, until golden, about 3 minutes.

To serve, place one pancake on each plate. Scoop ½ cup of the pork onto the pancake and garnish with ¼ cup coleslaw. Drizzle 3 tablespoons of the barbecue sauce on top.

Ham Hocks

BUSY BEE, OWNER TRACY GATES

Serves 3 to 4

The Busy Bee still serves this once-standard, now-disappearing meat-and-three staple—not as a bit of shredded meat in your greens, but a whole ham hock served as the main event. At the Busy Bee, they're as big as the Bronze Bomber's fist and pack just as powerful a wallop.

2 to 3 meaty smoked ham hocks

8 cups water

1/8 teaspoon liquid smoke

1/4 teaspoon white pepper

1/8 teaspoon Ac'cent (MSG)

1 teaspoon sugar

Salt

Combine all the ingredients in a large Dutch oven. Cover and bring to a boil. Reduce the heat and simmer for 2 hours, or until hocks are fork-tender. The longer the cooking time, the darker the skin and the greater the smoke flavoring will be.

Because of their size, you will need tongs to pick up and plate the ham hocks.

Paella de Verduras
Cuerno

Vegetables
Purloined Tomatoes

It was a rare night that I wasn't working—my fiancé and I were simply out for a romantic evening. The restaurant was one of the best in town, with a gorgeous environment and stunning view that made the evening seem as gilt-edged as the waitstaff's uniforms. The service was impressive, with a choreographed, simultaneous presentation of covered plates, their silver domes removed with a dramatic cymbal-like clash.

There was no menu. Instead, a stiff-backed waiter folded his white-gloved hands behind his back, stared heavenward and began to recite the long, fanciful names of the Continental specialties available that evening. Occasionally, he would glance at us to be sure we were salivating—and we were—but it wasn't until he listed one item that I had to stop him. "The chef is also making a salad of purloined tomatoes," the waiter intoned, moving swiftly into the involved preparation.

"Wait," I said. "Did you say 'purloined' tomatoes?"

"They are specially grown tomatoes," the waiter said, with the bored tone of the learned teaching the uninformed, "with

the seeds harvested and saved from one generation to the next . . . "

"Doesn't 'purloined' mean 'stolen'?" I asked.

"Well, stolen fruit is more delicious," my fiancé offered.

"Are you sure you don't mean heirloom tomatoes?" I asked.

There was a short pause, as the waiter's eyes seemed to search the ceiling for his missing Teleprompter. "Yes!" he said abruptly, meeting our eyes for the first time, "That is what they are!" He had the relieved tone of someone who'd been handed the cell phone he'd left in a taxi. Local ingredients were clearly a new introduction in this thoroughly traditional "fine dining" environment.

I hardly remember anything else we had for dinner that night, but the tomato salad was so good it might have been made from stolen fruit. The best Southern vegetables taste as though they might have been picked that day. Like a good meat-and-three, we're offering plenty of options to go with your main dish—or perhaps you'd prefer a vegetable plate?

Heirloom Tomatoes

BABETTE'S CAFÉ, CHEF/OWNER MARLA ADAMS

Serves 6

Homegrown tomatoes conjure the season like no other vegetable (or, more accurately, fruit). Just as a mere touch of mascara and lip gloss can turn natural beauties into stunners, chef Marla Adams needs only a splash of oil, vinegar, and herbs to make you want to crown these with a tiara.

2½ to 3 pounds heirloom tomatoes, sliced ¼ inch thick

2 tablespoons extra virgin olive oil

2 tablespoons aged balsamic vinegar

1 teaspoon sea salt

Freshly ground black pepper

3 tablespoons thinly sliced basil

Arrange the tomatoes on a plate. Drizzle with the olive oil and vinegar. Sprinkle with the salt, pepper, and basil, and serve.

Collard Greens

WAHOO!, CHEF SCOTT WARREN

Serves 6 to 8

What's your definition of luxury? To me, it's having a score of Atlanta restaurants that proudly serve great collard greens—including this Decatur neighborhood favorite.

  2 tablespoons canola oil

  ½ yellow onion, diced

  1 rib celery, diced

  ½ red bell pepper, diced

  1 jalapeño, diced

  1 pound collard greens, washed and chopped (stems can be diced into ¼-inch pieces and added to mixture)

  4 quarts water

  6 tablespoons apple cider vinegar

  ⅓ cup honey

  1 teaspoon dried red pepper flakes

  2 tablespoons salt

Heat the oil in a large pot over medium-high heat. Add the onion, celery, bell pepper, and jalapeño. Add the collards, water, vinegar, honey, red pepper, and salt and bring to a boil. Turn down the heat to a simmer and cook for 1½ hours, or until the collards are tender. Add liquid as needed if the water reduces too much. Serve hot.

Collard Greens

WISTERIA, CHEF JASON HILL

Serves 4

Chef Jason Hill's menu is seasonal—but the delicious collards are year-round staples.

  ¼ cup cubed bacon or back fat (salt pork)

  1 bunch collards, tough stems discarded and coarsely chopped, or 1 (1-pound) package of cleaned and chopped collards

  ½ onion, diced

  Pinch dried red pepper flakes

  ½ cup champagne vinegar

  ½ cup red wine vinegar

  4 cups water

  White pepper

  Salt

In a large saucepan over medium heat, cook the bacon until most of the fat is cooked out. Add the collards, onion, red pepper, champagne vinegar, wine vinegar, water, and white pepper to taste. Cover and cook until tender, about 1 hour. Add salt to taste; scoop and serve.

Fried Okra

CAKES & ALE, OWNERS BILLY AND KRISTIN ALLIN

Serves 4

"You can have strip pokra," wrote Roy Blount Jr. "Give me a nice girl and a dish of okra." Although I'll take it any way I can get it—stewed, simmered, roasted, braised—this lacy-edged fried cornmeal recipe is the crowd-pleasing favorite. (Nice girl not included.)

Ranch Dressing

½ cup mayonnaise

¼ cup crème fraîche

2 tablespoons buttermilk, or as needed

1 clove garlic, pounded into a paste

Salt and freshly ground black pepper

Okra

8 ounces okra, cut in half lengthwise

Vegetable oil, for deep-frying

1 cup medium-grind cornmeal

½ cup flour

1 teaspoon kosher salt

To make the dressing, combine the mayonnaise, crème fraîche, buttermilk, and garlic. Add salt and pepper to taste. Add additional buttermilk if needed to thin.

To prepare the okra, soak the cut okra in cold water for 5 minutes. Drain well.

Pour 4 to 6 inches of oil in a tall saucepan or deep-fryer and heat to 375 degrees F. It is important to use a large enough pot so that the oil fills it only halfway.

Combine the cornmeal, flour, and salt in a bowl. Add the okra and toss to coat. Fry the okra in the hot oil until golden. Drain well.

Serve the fried okra with the ranch dressing.

Golden Tomato Water

PARK 75 AT THE FOUR SEASONS,
CHEF ROBERT GERSTENECKER

Serves 4 to 6

*Known for their milder, less acidic taste, yellow tomatoes make a gorgeous
cold summer soup.*

Tomato Water

5 yellow tomatoes, quartered

1 cucumber, peeled
  and seeded

½ yellow bell pepper

½ red bell pepper

1 clove garlic

5 basil leaves

3 cilantro stems

2 tablespoons sherry vinegar

¼ cup olive oil

Salt and freshly ground
  black pepper

To Finish

4 tablespoons diced tomatoes

½ avocado, diced

4 basil leaves, diced

4 tablespoons extra virgin
  olive oil

Pinch sea salt

To prepare the tomato water, combine the quartered tomatoes, cucumber, yellow and red bell peppers, garlic, basil, cilantro, vinegar, and olive oil in a food processor. Puree until smooth. Season with salt and pepper.

Line a large sieve with cheesecloth and place on top of a tall nonreactive pot. Pour the tomato puree into center of cheesecloth. Gather the sides of the cheesecloth up over puree to form a large sack and, without squeezing puree, gently gather together cheesecloth to form a neck. Tie the neck securely with kitchen string. Tie the sack to a wooden spoon longer than diameter of the pot and remove sieve. Put the spoon across top of pot, suspending the sack inside pot and leaving enough room underneath the sack so that it will not sit in the tomato water that accumulates. Let the sack hang in refrigerator for at least 8 hours without ever squeezing the sack.

To finish, transfer the tomato water to a bowl and discard the sack and its contents. Garnish with the diced tomatoes, avocado, and basil. Finish with a drizzle of olive oil and a sprinkling of salt.

Woodland Gardens Cucumber and Pickled Cherry Tomato Salad with Cucumber Gelée and Ginger Rice Wine Vinaigrette

THE ATLANTA GRILL, CHEF BENNETT HOLLBERG

Serves 4

Fresh from the organic fields of Woodland Gardens in Winterville, Georgia, these tomatoes star in an elegant, deconstructed version of gazpacho.

Pickled Cherry Tomatoes

- 1 pint cherry tomatoes
- 2 cups rice vinegar
- 3 tablespoons mixed pickling spice
- 1 cup mirin
- 1 cup sugar

Cucumber Gelée

- 7 ounces European cucumber
- 1 gelatin sheet or ¾ teaspoon unflavored gelatin powder
- 2 tablespoons rice vinegar, plus more as needed
- ¼ teaspoon salt, plus more as needed
- 1¼ teaspoons sugar, plus more as needed

Salad

- 2 heirloom tomatoes, sliced ¼ to ⅓ inch thick
- Fleur de sel or other sea salt
- Freshly ground black pepper
- 1 tablespoon extra virgin olive oil
- ½ European cucumber, halved and sliced ⅛ inch thick

To prepare the pickled cherry tomatoes, score the bottom of each tomato with the tip of a paring knife. Dip the tomatoes into a pot of salted boiling water for 5 to 10 seconds, then immediately remove and put in ice water. When cool, drain the tomatoes and carefully remove the skin from each tomato using a paring knife.

Combine the rice vinegar, mirin, sugar, and pickling spice in a saucepan and bring to a boil. Simmer for 5 minutes, remove from

continued on page 156

heat, cover, and let cool at room temperature; then strain. Pour over the cherry tomatoes and refrigerate overnight.

To prepare the cucumber gelée, peel, seed, and chop the cucumbers into 1- to 2-inch pieces. Soften the gelatin sheet by submerging it for 5 minutes in enough ice water to cover. Heat the vinegar with the salt and sugar, stirring to dissolve the sugar. Stir in bloomed gelatin sheet or powdered gelatin mixture. Continue stirring until the gelatin dissolves.

If using powdered gelatin, sprinkle into cold vinegar then slowly heat while stirring until dissolved, making sure not to boil.

Transfer the cucumbers to a blender and puree on high speed until smooth. Pour into a mixing bowl over an ice bath and add the gelatin mixture. Stir to cool quickly. Taste and adjust seasoning with salt, sugar, and vinegar, if necessary. When cool, the gelée should have the consistency of loose Jell-O. Use a small spoon or pour into a squeeze bottle to put on the plate.

To prepare the salad, season the tomatoes with fleur de sel and pepper and drizzle with olive oil.

Cut two-thirds of the sliced cucumbers into thin half moons and add to the pickling liquid with the tomatoes. Place a slice of tomato in the center of the plate, then arrange the half moon slices of cucumber, slightly overlapping, around the outer edge of the tomato. Place another slice of tomato on top of the cucumber and repeat with the half moons of cucumber. Place a final slice of tomato on top of the cucumbers and arrange 5 full slices of cucumber on top of the tomato. Place the cucumber gelée around the base of the salad. Cut the pickled cherry tomatoes in half and arrange around the outside of the gelée and place a few on top of the salad and serve.

Pecan Wild Rice

REPAST, CHEF JOE TRUEX

Serves 8

A perfect accompaniment for quail or any other game dish—or, for that matter, as the centerpiece of a vegetable plate.

4½ cups chicken broth

2 cups uncooked wild rice

1½ tablespoons butter

2 teaspoons olive oil

½ cup chopped pecans

2 shallots, diced

3 tablespoons finely chopped fresh flat-leaf parsley

¾ teaspoon salt

¼ teaspoon freshly ground black pepper

Combine the broth and wild rice in a stock pot and bring to a boil. Cover, decrease the heat, and simmer for 1 hour, or until the wild rice is tender. Drain, transfer the rice to a bowl, and set aside.

Melt the butter and olive oil in a medium saucepan over medium-high heat. Add the pecans and shallots and sauté for 1 minute, or until the pecans are lightly toasted. Add the wild rice and parsley; mix thoroughly. Season with salt and pepper and serve.

Spaghetti Squash Salad with Aged Ricotta and Toasted Walnuts

SHORTY'S, OWNERS BRYAN WILSON, BRIAN HOGAN, AND MICHAEL MURPHY

Serves 4 to 6

Who would expect a hip little pizza joint to offer such an uptown dish? The savvy regulars at Shorty's, that's who.

2 medium spaghetti squash, halved and seeded

Olive oil

Salt and freshly ground black pepper

8 ounces baby arugula

1 lemon, cut into wedges

½ cup toasted walnuts

½ cup grated ricotta salata

½ cup diced plum tomatoes

Preheat the oven to 400 degrees F.

Coat the inside of the squash with olive oil and sprinkle with salt and pepper. Place squash skin-side down on a baking sheet and bake 30–40 minutes, until the squash is tender. Let cool.

Scrape the flesh from the skin and put into a bowl. Refrigerate for 1 hour.

Place a handful of baby arugula on the center of each plate. For each plate, toss 1 cup of squash with 1 tablespoon olive oil, salt and pepper, and the juice of a lemon wedge. Mound the mixture in the middle of the arugula. Sprinkle the top of the salad with 1½ to 2 tablespoons toasted walnuts, 1½ to 2 tablespoons grated ricotta salata, and 1½ to 2 tablespoons diced tomatoes.

Vegetable Biryani
HIMALAYAS, OWNERS MOIZ UDDIN AND ATAUR RAHMAN

Serves 6

This classic Indian dish recalls the riches of our own coastal regions, with rice, vegetables, and curry powder.

4 quarts water

6 tablespoons vegetable oil, divided

1¼ teaspoons salt, divided

1 cup basmati rice

1½ teaspoons cumin seeds

1 large onion, chopped

1 tablespoon ground turmeric

1 tablespoon yellow curry powder

1 pound assorted fresh vegetables, including broccoli, green bell peppers, zucchini, potato, squash, carrots, and string beans

¼ cup fresh cilantro, chopped

Combine water, 1 tablespoon oil, and ¼ teaspoon salt in a large pot. Bring to a boil and add the rice. Cover and continue to boil for 10 minutes. To test for doneness, remove a few grains of rice. Press the rice; if they are soft, then the rice is cooked. If not, continue cooking for 1 to 2 minutes and retest. When the rice is cooked, drain off the water and set rice aside.

Meanwhile, heat the remaining vegetable oil in large pan over high heat. Add the cumin seeds, mix well, and then add the onions. Sauté, stirring, until mixture is light brown. Add the turmeric, curry, remaining salt, and vegetables. Cook until the vegetables are soft, or to your taste.

Add the cooked rice to the vegetable mixture and mix well.

Serve mounded on a large plate, garnished with the fresh cilantro.

Butter Bean and Corn Succotash

EUGENE, CHEF/OWNER LINTON HOPKINS

Serves 8

Standard on any Southern table, succotash was often a humble composition of canned and frozen limas and corn. Chef Linton Hopkins makes it a rich lietmotif of fresh vegetables.

8 cups water

2 tablespoons salt

2 cups fresh green butter beans or lima beans

2 tablespoons butter

1 small Vidalia onion, finely diced

1 clove garlic

2 cups uncooked corn kernels

$1/2$ cup chicken stock

$1/2$ cup heavy cream

Salt and freshly ground black pepper

$1/4$ cup chopped fresh parsley

Bring the water and salt to a rolling boil. Add the butter beans and cook until tender, 20–30 minutes. Drain. Shock in ice water to quickly stop the cooking. Set aside.

Melt the butter in a medium saucepan over medium heat. Add the onion and sauté until soft, about 5 minutes. Add the garlic and cook until fragrant, 30 seconds. Add the corn and then the stock; cook until the stock is reduced to a glaze. Toss in the butter beans and cream; reduce to a glaze. Season to taste with salt and pepper, sprinkle with parsley, and serve hot.

Sharon Carver's Rutabagas

CARVER'S COUNTRY KITCHEN,
OWNERS ROBERT AND SHARON CARVER

Serves 6

Who else can take everybody's least-favorite root vegetable and make it something simply grand? Sharon Carver, of course, queen of the old-fashioned meat-and-three.

3 large rutabagas, peeled and diced
1/3 cup butter, melted, or to taste
1/2 cup sugar, or to taste
Salt and freshly ground black pepper
Onion powder

Add the rutabagas to a pan of salted water and bring to a boil. Cook until fork-tender, about 45 minutes. Drain well and transfer to a bowl. Mix in the butter and sugar. Season to taste with salt and pepper and onion powder. Mix thoroughly but do not mash.

When adding the seasonings to the cooked diced rutabagas, start out with small amounts until you reach the desired taste.

Pot Likker

MARY MAC'S TEA ROOM, OWNER JOHN FERRELL

Makes 6 to 8 cups

It's a kind of baptism by greens: first-time visitors to Mary Mac's are still treated to a complimentary cup of this intoxicating brew, a kind of pork-spiked vegetable broth from cooking turnip greens, along with cracklin' cornbread. The first taste is always free, isn't it?

1 ounce fatback, cubed

2 cups chicken stock

2 cups water (or chicken broth for a richer soup)

1 cup cooked turnip greens and juice

Salt and freshly ground white pepper

Dash hot sauce or pepper vinegar

Fry the fatback in a heavy frying pan over medium heat, taking care not to burn the drippings. Transfer the fatback and drippings to a 3-quart stock pot.

In the pot, add the chicken stock, water, and cooked greens and juice. Simmer at least 5 minutes. Taste and season with salt, freshly ground white pepper, and a dash of hot sauce or pepper vinegar. Serve hot.

French Fries with Pepper Gravy

VICKERY'S BAR AND GRILL, OWNERS CHIP
NEY, SAM WEYMAN, AND JERRY NAGLER

Serves 12

Don't knock it till you've tried it: the Vickery's hand-cut, unpeeled fries are nearly a full meal when dipped into this pepper-flecked gravy.

Roux

¼ cup flour

¼ to ½ cup melted
  clarified butter

Potatoes

12 baking or Idaho Burbank
  potatoes, raw and unpeeled

Oil for deep-frying

Salt

Gravy

4 cups water

2 tablespoons beef base paste

1 teaspoon Kitchen Bouquet or
  other gravy browning sauce

6 tablespoons roux

2 tablespoons cracked
  black pepper

To make the roux, heat pan on medium to medium-high heat, add flour and butter, and cook 2–4 minutes.

To make the gravy, combine the water, beef base, and Kitchen Bouquet in a saucepan and bring to a boil. Whisk slowly while adding roux a tablespoon at a time. Remove from the heat and add the pepper. Keep warm.

To make the French fries, cut the potatoes a day ahead of time. Cut to a ³⁄₈-inch julienne, using a mandolin or similar cutting tool. Soak overnight in cold water. When you are ready to cook, heat the oil in a tall pot or deep-fryer to 350 degrees F. Add the potatoes and fry in oil until golden brown and crispy. Drain and salt to taste.

Serve hot with the gravy poured over the fries.

Turnip Greens and Cornbread Muffins

MARY MAC'S TEA ROOM, OWNER JOHN FERRELL

Makes 4 servings

Now that you're hooked on Mary Mac's pot likker, you're likely going to want to go on to stronger stuff—like these robust turnip greens.

A longtime favorite Southern green vegetable, turnip greens are leafier and slightly more bitter than collards. Watch out for insects, which love turnip greens too. Wash through three or more changes of water, until the last water is clear and free of sand.

Turnip Greens

- 4 ounces fatback (salt pork), thinly sliced
- 4 cups water
- 2 teaspoons salt
- 1 teaspoon freshly ground white pepper
- 2 pounds turnip greens, stems removed
- 1 cup chicken stock
- 1 tablespoon chicken fat (saved from top of chicken stock), melted (optional)
- Pinch of sugar (optional)

Muffins

Makes 24

- 1 egg
- 1 cup buttermilk
- 1 tablespoon sugar
- 1/8 teaspoon salt
- 1/4 cup melted lard or vegetable shortening
- 1 cup Martha White cornmeal mix
- 1/4 cup Martha White self-rising flour
- 1 tablespoon baking powder

Put the fatback in a large heavy pot and fry until crisp. Add the water, salt, and white pepper and bring to a boil. Add the greens, stirring them down as they wilt. Cover and simmer briskly for about 1 hour. Remove the greens, chop, and return to saucepan.

At this point, the greens may be cooled and stored in their broth in the refrigerator until you plan to serve them.

To make the cornbread muffins, beat egg well and add the buttermilk, sugar, salt, and lard. Mix well. Add to this mixture the cornmeal mix, flour, and baking powder and mix lightly. Do not beat.

Preheat the oven to 450 degrees F.

Measure 2 heaping tablespoons of mixture into a well-greased muffin cup pan, filling almost to the top. It is not necessary to heat the muffin tins first if you use a very hot oven.

Bake the muffins for 15–18 minutes.

To serve, bring the pot of greens back to a boil and add the chicken stock. Simmer, covered, for 30 minutes. Taste and correct the seasonings. If greens are unusually bitter, add the chicken fat, or try a very small amount of sugar. Serve hot with crumbled cornbread muffins.

Sweet Potato Fries with Tasmanian Pepperberry Sauce

THE VORTEX BAR & GRILL, OWNERS HANK, MICHAEL, AND SUZANNE BENOIT

Serves 4

Not to be outdone by the Vickery's fries and pepper gravy, this burger joint offers an even richer duo.

Tasmanian Pepperberry Sauce

- 1 cup Pepperberry Seasoning (available at www.bushdreams.ca)
- 1 cup dark brown sugar
- 2 tablespoons water
- 1½ cups mayonnaise

Oven-Baked Sweet Potato Fries

- 1½ pounds sweet potatoes, peeled and cut into ½-inch strips
- ¼ cup olive oil
- 1½ teaspoons kosher salt

To prepare the sauce, mix together the Pepperberry Seasoning, brown sugar, water, and mayonnaise. Refrigerate 2 hours.

Preheat the oven to 425 degrees F. Line a baking sheet with aluminum foil.

To prepare the oven fries, toss sweet potatoes with olive oil and sprinkle with salt. Spread out the cut sweet potatoes evenly on the lined baking sheet. Bake for 30 minutes, until brown.

Serve immediately, passing the pepperberry sauce on the side.

Sweet Potato French Fries

Oven-baked fries are easier for the home cook to make, but if you prefer to French-fry the sweet potatoes, then use this recipe.

- 4 cups peanut oil
- 4 medium sweet potatoes, peeled

Heat the oil to 350 degrees F in a deep skillet or deep-fat fryer.
Cut the sweet potatoes into ¾-inch strips. For best results, use

a crinkle-cut attachment on a food processor.

Test the oil by dropping a fry into it—it should sizzle when it is ready. Drop the sweet potatoes in small batches into the hot oil to avoid clumping. Cook for 5 to 10 minutes, according to the doneness you prefer. The potatoes should be golden orange on the outside and tender on the inside. Remove from the oil and pat dry with a paper towel.

Paella de Verduras

CUERNO, OWNER RICCARDO ULLIO

Serves 6

A one-dish, full-meal alternative to Cuerno's traditional meat-and-seafood combinations, this recipe is a legacy of the departed restaurant's specialty.

Paella

1/4 cup Spanish olive oil

4 cloves garlic, finely minced

1/2 head cauliflower, broken into florets

1 bunch white asparagus, thinly sliced

1/2 cup English (green) peas, fresh or frozen

1/2 cup fresh shelled fava beans

4 piquillo peppers, cut into thin strips

4 artichoke hearts, cut into quarters

1 tomato, peeled, seeded, and diced

2 cups medium-grain rice

4 cups vegetable broth

Salt and freshly ground black pepper

1/8 teaspoon smoked paprika (pimenton)

Pinch saffron threads

Lemon wedges, to serve

Preheat the oven to 425 degrees F.

Heat the olive oil in a paella pan or ovenproof skillet over medium-high heat. Add the garlic and sauté until browned. Add the cauliflower, asparagus, peas, fava beans, piquillo peppers, artichokes, and tomato and cook until lightly colored. Stir in the rice. Add in vegetable broth; season with salt and pepper, paprika, and saffron. Give one final stir and then bring to a simmer. Simmer ten minutes, stirring occasionally.

Transfer the pan to the oven and bake for 8 minutes.

Remove from the oven and let cool for 5 minutes. Serve with lemon wedges.

Beet Salad

WISTERIA, CHEF JASON HILL

Serves 4 to 6

All good Southerners love beets, especially in a colorful, cold summer salad splashed with fig vinaigrette and enriched with candied walnuts.

Salad

1 red beet

1 golden beet

8 cups water

$\frac{1}{2}$ cup red wine vinegar

4 teaspoons salt

Balsamic Candied Walnuts

2 tablespoons vegetable oil

$\frac{1}{2}$ cup walnuts

2 tablespoons balsamic vinegar

1 tablespoon sugar

Pinch ground cinnamon

Pinch ground cloves

Golden Fig Vinaigrette

6 ounces dried golden figs

$1\frac{1}{2}$ cups champagne vinegar

$\frac{1}{2}$ cup red wine vinegar

$\frac{1}{4}$ cup sugar

2 tablespoons molasses

1 tablespoon minced garlic

To Finish

1 ($\frac{1}{2}$-pound bag) baby arugula

1 to 2 oranges, peeled, seeded, and divided into segments

Feta cheese, crumbled

To prepare the salad, place each beet in a separate saucepan. Add 4 cups water, $\frac{1}{4}$ cup red wine vinegar, and 2 teaspoons salt to each. Bring to a boil and boil until tender, 30–60 minutes, depending on the size of the beet. Let cool. Rub off the skins with your hands under water while the beets are still warm. Julienne slice into $\frac{1}{8}$-inch matchsticks.

To prepare the candied walnuts, heat the oil in a medium sauté pan over medium heat. Add the walnuts and sauté until fragrant and lightly toasted. Deglaze the pan with the vinegar, stirring with a wooden spoon until the vinegar starts to bind to the walnuts. Add the sugar, cinnamon, and cloves and toss with spoon until sugar caramelizes. Continue until the walnuts are candied (the sugar sticks to the nuts and is no longer grainy). Set aside to cool.

To prepare the vinaigrette, combine the figs, vinegars, sugar,

molasses, and garlic in a saucepan and bring to a simmer for 5 minutes. Let cool slightly. Puree in a blender until smooth. If the mixture is too thick, add more water and champagne vinegar until the mixture has the consistency of a ranch-style dressing.

To assemble the salad, combine the arugula, beets, oranges, and walnuts. Add the vinaigrette. Toss lightly. Top with feta cheese, using as little or as much as you like.

Tomato Aspic

THE COLONNADE, CHEF RYAN COBB

Serves 20

Bastion of old-school Southern meats, vegetables, yeast rolls, highballs, and waitresses who call you "hon," the Colonnade has been serving traditional dishes like this tomato aspic for more than eight decades.

8 (¼-ounce) envelopes unflavored gelatin

6 cups Bloody Mary mix

⅓ cup finely diced onion

1 rib celery, finely diced

4 cups hot water

Homemade mayonnaise, to garnish

Parsley, to garnish

Sprinkle the gelatin over the Bloody Mary mix and let soften (bloom) for 2 minutes.

In a separate bowl, combine the onion, celery, and hot water. Add the Bloody Mary and gelatin mixture and mix well. Pour into twenty 3½-ounce molds. Refrigerate overnight.

To serve, dip the molds into hot water and invert onto serving plates. Garnish with mayonnaise and parsley and serve at once.

Corn Pudding

WISTERIA, CHEF JASON HILL

Serves 8

Here's what to make of all that garden corn you froze last summer.

1⅓ cups frozen and thawed or fresh corn
    kernels (frozen works the best)

1½ cups rice flour

2½ teaspoons baking powder

2 teaspoons salt

½ cup butter, melted

½ cup buttermilk

¾ cup sugar

3 large whole eggs, beaten

Preheat the oven to 350 degrees F. Lightly grease a 9 x 13-inch baking dish.

Puree the corn in a food processor. Set aside.

Mix together the rice flour, baking powder, and salt in a bowl.

In a separate bowl, mix together the pureed corn, butter, buttermilk, and sugar. Mix in the dry ingredients. Gently fold in the eggs. Transfer to the prepared baking dish. Bake 30 minutes, or until the top is golden brown and a toothpick inserted in the center comes out clean. Serve hot.

Sweet Potato Casserole

CARVER'S COUNTRY KITCHEN,
OWNERS ROBERT AND SHARON CARVER

Serves 6 to 8

On the other hand, when gilding the lily is called for, Sharon Carver succeeds at that as well. As we all know, nothing succeeds like excess. Here it is, in its brown-sugar-enhanced glory.

3 cups mashed cooked fresh or
    canned sweet potatoes

1 cup sugar

2 large eggs

1/2 cup butter, melted

1/2 cup evaporated milk

1 teaspoon vanilla extract

1 teaspoon rum flavoring

2 teaspoons ground cinnamon or pumpkin pie spice

Pecan Topping

1 cup chopped pecans

1 cup brown sugar

1/3 cup flour

1/3 cup butter, at room temperature

Preheat the oven to 350 degrees F. Grease a 1-quart casserole dish.

Mix together the sweet potatoes, sugar, eggs, butter, evaporated milk, vanilla, rum flavoring, and cinnamon in large bowl. Beat with an electric mixer just until blended. Pour into the prepared casserole dish.

To make the topping, mix together the pecans, brown sugar, flour, and butter until crumbly. Sprinkle on top of the casserole.

Bake for 30 minutes or until set. Serve hot.

Bailey's Soufflé with Mocha Chocolate Chip Crème Fraîche
Nikolai's Roof

Desserts

The Sweet Life

Does anything represent Southern living better than our desserts? Oh, we've got it sweet here. For all our past strife, our Atlanta present sometimes feels perfect. Great weather, beautiful landscape—and despite our big-city ways, we still have some of our old-fashioned habits. We take things a little slower. You can sit at a green light for at least two seconds without anyone honking. We're more likely to nod and say hello to passersby. We may suddenly pretend we're good friends with a perfect stranger to share a laugh. And when we do find something to laugh about—very often ourselves—we laugh the unrestricted belly laugh of the guiltless sinner. Hey—no one's perfect, least of all us. Maybe that's why Southern churchgoers sin so blatantly at their reunions and suppers, giving in to their deadly weaknesses for pecan pie or lemon pound cake with absolute abandon. You might have had chocolate cake before, but not like we've got here—it's more deeply chocolate with a thick overcoat of frosting just begging for a glass of milk. What would any Southern gathering be without eating just a little too much, laughing a little too hard, and hearing some sweet old music before heading back to the sideboard for just one more bite of hummingbird cake?

Grilled Lemon Pound Cake with Key Lime Butter Cookie Gelato

DOGWOOD, CHEF SHANE TOUHY

Serves 10 to 12

This cake is as pretty as the interior of this downtown restaurant.

Pound Cake

1¼ cups unsalted butter,
    at room temperature

1½ cups sugar

2¼ cups flour

6 large eggs

1 teaspoon vanilla extract

1 teaspoon lemon extract

1 teaspoon almond extract

Finely grated zest and
    juice of 1 lemon

Lemon Simple Syrup

1 cup water

1 cup sugar

1 tablespoon freshly
    squeezed lemon juice

To Serve

Fresh strawberries, hulled
    and sliced

Mint leaves

Ice cream or gelato (use
    Greenwood Regional's
    "Jake's Key Lime–Butter
    Cookie" or substitute
    your favorite flavor)

Preheat the oven to 325 degrees F. Grease a 1-quart loaf pan or a 4-cup loaf pan of any shape.

To prepare the cake, cream together the butter and sugar until light and smooth. Add the flour a little at a time until fully incorporated. Be sure to scrape down the sides of the bowl as you go. Add the eggs one at a time, beating until fully incorporated. Add the vanilla, lemon, and almond extracts, lemon zest, and lemon juice. Continue to mix until smooth. Transfer to the prepared loaf pan.

Bake 45 to 50 minutes, until a toothpick inserted into the center comes out clean. Cool completely in the pan on a wire rack.

While the cake cools, prepare the lemon simple syrup. Combine the water, sugar, and lemon juice and cook 3 to 4 minutes, until the mixture thickens to a syrupy consistency. Allow to cool.

Use a long, thin knife to loosen the sides of the cake from the pan. Remove the cake from the pan and cut it into ½-inch-thick slices. Generously brush the lemon syrup on the face of each slice.

Heat a grill or griddle over medium heat. Lightly grill the slices just long enough to get some grill marks, about 10 seconds. Then rotate and grill 10 seconds more.

Serve two slices, topped with a couple of slices of fresh strawberries, mint, and a scoop of ice cream.

Georgia Peach Tart Tatin
THE GLOBE

Serves 4

The late, beloved Globe served hipped-up Southern food to a beautiful crowd of tech-savvy young people. This recipe is the restaurant's final hat-tip to their former fans.

Tart

- 2 (9¼ x 9½-inch) sheets puff pastry, homemade or store-bought, thawed if frozen
- 6 to 8 Georgia white peaches
- Juice of 1 lemon
- 1 cup sugar
- 6 tablespoons unsalted butter, diced

Ice cream

- 2 cups heavy cream
- ½ vanilla bean
- ½ cup sugar
- 4 ounces basil, stems removed
- 6 large egg yolks

Chiffonade of fresh basil, to garnish

Preheat oven to 275 degrees F.

To prepare the tart, roll the puff pastry to ⅛-inch thickness and cut to just fit inside 4 (5-inch) tart pans, each with a removable bottom. Bake 10 minutes. Set aside to cool.

Lightly poach the peaches in boiling water for 1 minute and shock in ice water. Peel peaches and slice into 10 pieces each. Combine the lemon juice and sugar in a bowl and add the peaches. Toss lightly to coat. Let rest for 30 minutes.

Layer the peaches in the tart pans and top with the diced butter. Sprinkle the remaining sugar and juices over the peaches. Lower the heat to 175 degrees F and bake the tart until the peaches are soft and slightly caramelized, about 1 hour. Let cool overnight.

To make the ice cream, combine the cream, vanilla bean, sugar, and basil and bring to a boil. Remove from the heat and cover with the plastic wrap. Let stand for 30 minutes, then strain out the solids and discard. Slowly whisk the cream into the egg yolks and return to low heat. Stir constantly until thick. Remove from heat and chill. Freeze in an ice-cream maker according to the manufacturer's directions. To serve, preheat the oven to 375 degrees F. Remove the sides of the

tart pan and place the tart on a baking sheet. Heat until warm in the center, about 8 to 10 minutes. Place the tart in the center of a dessert plate and top with ice cream. Serve immediately, garnished with a chiffonade of basil.

Pecan Pie

THE PECAN, CHEF/OWNER TONY MORROW

Makes 1 pie

One sure way to find out where you're from: if you pronounce it "pe-KAHN," you're probably from the South. If you say "PEE-can," you probably never had this growing up.

2 cups dark corn syrup

1/2 cup unsalted butter

2 cups sugar

2 teaspoons vanilla extract

2 teaspoons salt

4 large eggs

1 (9-inch) standard pie shell

2 cups chopped pecans

Preheat the oven to 300 degrees F.

Combine the corn syrup and butter in a medium saucepan over low heat and cook until the butter is melted. Add the sugar, vanilla, and salt; mix well. Beat the eggs in a bowl. Slowly add the syrup mixture to the eggs, stirring constantly.

Fill the pie shell with the pecans. Pour the syrup mixture over top.

Bake for 45 minutes, or until the edges are set but the center is still soft. The pie will firm up as it cools. Let cool on a rack for at least 1 hour before serving.

Mango Pavlova

JOËL BRASSERIE, CHEF CYRILLE HOLOTA

Serves 8 to 10

Named for the Russian ballerina Anna Pavlova, this fruit-and-meringue dessert looks simple and elegant but requires as much practice and discipline as a pas de deux.

Sorbet

⅔ cup water

2¼ cups sugar

2 ounces pineapple paste or mango paste

1 vanilla bean

3 tablespoons orange juice

1 cup lemon juice

½ banana, mashed

Zest of 1 lemon

Pastry Cream

4 cups milk

7 egg yolks

¾ cup sugar

¾ cup flour

Meringue

1⅓ cups egg whites, or about 12 eggs

1¼ cups sugar

Mango Chutney

21 ounces fresh pineapple, finely diced

14 ounces mango, finely diced

2 ounces passion fruit, finely diced

½ cup sugar

To make the sorbet, combine the water and sugar in a medium saucepan and bring to a boil. Add the pineapple paste, vanilla bean, orange juice, lemon juice, and banana. Transfer to a blender and puree. Strain this mix and discard the solids. Stir in the lemon zest. Freeze in an ice-cream maker according to the manufacturer's directions. Store in the freezer until needed.

To make the meringues, preheat the oven to 250 degrees F. Line a baking sheet with parchment paper.

Whip the egg whites until foamy. Add the sugar and beat until stiff. Pipe the meringue mix into 8 to 10 (2½ ounces each) dome-shape mounds, each measuring about 3 inches in diameter. Bake the meringues for 1 hour, until firm. Cool to room temperature, then scoop out the meringues from the bottom until the domes are completely hollow. Be careful not to break them!

To make the mango chutney, combine the pineapple, mango, passion fruit, and sugar in a medium saucepan over medium-low heat. Cook till all water has evaporated. Refrigerate until cold.

To make the pastry cream, heat the milk to just simmering. In a bowl, beat together the egg yolks, sugar, and flour. Gradually add the hot milk, a tablespoon at a time, until about half of the milk has been added. Return everything to the pot and cook over low heat for 10 minutes, stirring constantly, until the mixture has thickened. Spread out the cream on a sheet pan and cover with plastic wrap. Refrigerate until very cold.

To serve, fill the meringues with the pastry cream, then the mango chutney, smoothing the top with a spatula. On one side of the plate place the pavlova flat side down, next to a little chutney. Place the sorbet on top of the pavlova with a little sauce spread around it.

NOTE: The chef says that weight measurement is used instead of volume here because of the fine dicing of the fruit. A kitchen scale is suggested.

Baklava Flogeres

KYMA, BUCKHEAD LIFE RESTAURANT GROUP

Makes 60 pieces

At Pano Karatassos's restaurant-tribute to his homeland, Greece, this light version of the traditional many-layered pastry, flecked with clove and cinnamon, is perfect with some potent Greek coffee.

To make this dessert you will need a saccharometer, which is a type of hydrometer that measures the amount of sugar in a solution. It is used primarily by winemakers, brewers, and confectioners. You will also need a 2-foot long metal dowel with a diameter $\frac{1}{32}$ of an inch.

Baklava Syrup

3⅓ cups sugar

¾ cup light corn syrup

Juice of 1½ lemons

1⅓ cups water

2 cinnamon sticks

3 whole cloves

Baklava Rolls

4 cups walnuts, finely chopped

1 cup dried bread crumbs

½ cup sugar

2¼ teaspoons ground cinnamon

1⅛ teaspoons ground cloves

1 (1–pound) box phyllo #4

4 cups butter, melted

To make the syrup, combine the sugar, corn syrup, lemon juice, and water in a large pot. Bring to a boil and allow to boil for 10 minutes. Pour into a tall container and allow to cool thoroughly, then chill in the refrigerator.

When the syrup is cool, measure the syrup's density with a saccharometer. The syrup should be at the 32 mark. If the syrup is over 32, add water little by little, testing after each addition until 32 is achieved. If the syrup happens to be less than 32, return the syrup to the heat and boil for 20 minutes. Then retest. If you don't have a saccharometer, then determine if the syrup is correct by seeing if it is as thin as natural maple syrup, but thinner then artificial syrup. Add the cloves and cinnamon sticks, and place the syrup in the refrigerator to chill.

To make the baklava rolls, preheat the oven to 350 degrees F. Lightly grease an 18 x 10 x 2-inch baking pan.

Mix together the walnuts, bread crumbs, sugar, cinnamon, and cloves. Take one sheet of phyllo. Brush with butter and fold the longer end over one edge just enough to completely cover the dowel. Sprinkle about ¼ cup of nut mixture evenly along the folded edge of the phyllo. Roll up the phyllo over the mixture until all the dough is around the dowel. Slide the dowel out of the roll. Scrunch both ends toward the middle of the roll gently. Place in the pan. Repeat until you have made 20 rolls. In the pan, cut each roll into thirds, about 2 inches each.

Bake the baklava rolls for 12 minutes, or until golden brown.

Pour the chilled baklava syrup over the hot baklava and let cool. Serve at room temperature.

Hummingbird Cake

SON'S PLACE, OWNER LENN STOREY

Serves 8 to 12

This cake with nuts, fruit, and cream cheese frosting has a mysterious name that no one seems able to trace. But since its appearance in the '60s, it quickly has become a fixture at church suppers and reunions. Sadly, Son's Place is now gone, but Lenn Storey's daughter's recipe remains.

3 cups flour

2 cups sugar

1 teaspoon plus 1 pinch salt, divided

1 teaspoon baking soda

1 teaspoon ground cinnamon

3 large eggs, beaten

1½ cups vegetable oil

3½ teaspoons vanilla extract, divided

1 (8-ounce) can crushed pineapple, undrained

2 cups chopped bananas

2 cups pecans, divided

2 (8-ounce) packages cream cheese, at room temperature

1 cup butter, at room temperature

2 (16-ounce) boxes confectioners' sugar

Preheat the oven to 350 degrees F. Grease and flour three 9-inch cake pans. Combine the flour, sugar, 1 teaspoon salt, baking soda, and cinnamon in a large bowl. Add the eggs and oil and stir until moistened. Stir in 1½ teaspoons vanilla extract, pineapple, bananas, and 1 cup pecans. Spoon the batter into the prepared cake pans.

Bake for 25 minutes, or until toothpicks inserted in centers of the cakes come out clean. Cool the cakes in the pans on wire racks for 10 minutes. Remove the cakes from the pans and cool completely on wire racks.

Meanwhile, prepare frosting. In large bowl with an electric mixer at medium speed, beat cream cheese and butter until smooth. Add confectioners' sugar and beat until light and fluffy. Stir in the remaining vanilla and remaining salt.

Spread the frosting between layers, on the sides, and on top of the cake. Garnish with the remaining pecans.

Southern Pecan Pie with Ginger Whipped Cream

WISTERIA, CHEF JASON HILL

Serves 8

Sweet, snappy, cool, hot, crunchy, and gooey, Wisteria's version of the Georgia classic covers all the bases.

Pecan Pie

- 1¼ cups pecans: 1 cup coarsely chopped, ¼ cup whole
- 1 (9-inch) pie shell, chilled
- 3 large eggs, lightly beaten
- 1 cup light corn syrup
- ¼ cup dark brown sugar
- 1 tablespoon Grandma's Original molasses
- 2 tablespoons unsalted butter, melted
- 2 tablespoons flour
- ¼ teaspoon salt
- 1 teaspoon vanilla extract (Mexican vanilla is best)

Ginger Whipped Cream

- 1 cup heavy cream
- 1 tablespoon confectioners' sugar
- 1 teaspoon ground ginger, or 1 tablespoon chopped pickled ginger

Preheat the oven to 375 degrees F.

Spread the pecans along the bottom of the pie shell.

Combine eggs, corn syrup, brown sugar, molasses, butter, flour, salt, and vanilla in a bowl. Pour over the pecans. (The pecans will rise to the top of the pie.)

Bake for 45–50 minutes, until the filling has set. (About 20 minutes into baking you may wish to tent the edges of the pie crust with aluminum foil to prevent the pie crust edges from burning.) Remove from the oven and let cool completely.

To prepare the whipped cream, combine the cream, confectioners' sugar, and ginger in a standing mixer and beat until the cream has almost doubled in volume and will form firm peaks.

Pipe the whipped cream over the pie and serve.

Churros

HOLY TACO, CHEF/OWNER ROBERT PHALEN

Serves 8 to 10

Mmmmm. . . . The Mexican version of the cinnamon-crusted doughnut is usually dunked in hot chocolate—but here it is served with its own chocolate sauce.

5 cups water

1 cup unsalted butter

2 teaspoons salt

1/2 cup sugar

1/2 cup vegetable oil

2 teaspoons Frangelico (hazelnut liqueur)

1 teaspoon ground cinnamon

5 cups flour

8 large eggs, lightly beaten

Vegetable oil, for deep-frying

Cinnamon-Sugar

1/2 cup sugar

1/2 cup ground cinnamon

Chocolate Sauce

4 cups heavy cream

1/2 pound Mexican chocolate, chopped

To make the churros, combine the water, butter, salt, sugar, oil, Frangelico, and cinnamon in a large saucepan. Bring to a rolling boil. Stir in the flour and continue to stir vigorously over low heat until the mixture forms a ball, about 1 minute.

Remove from the heat and beat in the eggs all at once. Continue beating until smooth. Let the dough cool. Put the dough into a piping bag fitted with a star tip.

To make the cinnamon-sugar, combine the cinnamon and sugar in bowl and mix well.

To make the chocolate sauce, bring the cream to a boil. Pour over the chocolate and stir until the chocolate is melted.

Pour 2 to 3 inches of vegetable oil, or enough for the dough to be submerged, into a large frying pan and heat to 350 degrees F. Pipe the churros in long rods directly into the hot oil. Fry until golden brown on all sides. Dust with the cinnamon-sugar and serve with chocolate sauce.

Orange Buttermilk Chess Pie

SOUTH CITY KITCHEN, OWNER DEAN DUPUIS

Serves 8

Sweet, tart, and tangy: the perfect combination for a cool-of-the-evening summer dessert.

4 large eggs, beaten
2 cups sugar
1 tablespoon cornmeal
1 tablespoon flour
1/2 teaspoon salt
1/4 cup unsalted butter, melted and cooled
1/4 cup buttermilk
1 1/2 tablespoons freshly squeezed orange juice
1 1/2 tablespoons freshly squeezed lemon juice
3 tablespoons apple cider vinegar
1 tablespoon finely grated orange zest
1 1/2 teaspoons vanilla extract
1 (9-inch) pie shell

Preheat the oven to 325 degrees F.

Whisk together the eggs, sugar, cornmeal, and flour in a large bowl until well combined. Add the salt, butter, buttermilk, orange juice, lemon juice, vinegar, orange zest, and vanilla; whisk until fully combined. Pour into the pie shell.

Bake for 20 minutes. Rotate the pie, reduce heat to 300 degrees F, and bake 20 to 30 minutes more, or until firm and slightly brown.

Cool completely before serving.

Manchego Cheesecake with Strawberry Fennel Compote

REPAST, CHEF JOE TRUEX

Serves 8

Manchego, the distinctive sheep's milk cheese, makes a unique cheesecake and is topped here with a rich fruit-and-fennel compote.

White Sponge Cake Base

- 8 large eggs
- 1¼ cups sugar
- 1¾ cups plus 1 tablespoon pastry flour
- ⅓ cup unsalted butter, melted
- Dash vanilla extract
- Pinch salt

Manchego Cheese Filling

- 12 ounces cream cheese, at room temperature
- 10 ounces manchego cheese, grated
- ¼ cup milk
- ½ cup unsalted butter, at room temperature
- 5 large egg whites
- 1 teaspoon cream of tartar
- ⅔ cup plus ¼ cup sugar, divided
- 5 large egg yolks
- ¼ cup honey
- 2 tablespoons freshly squeezed lemon juice
- ¼ cup plus 1 teaspoon cornstarch

Strawberry Compote

- 1 teaspoon fennel seeds
- 1 cup sugar
- Juice of 1 lemon
- 2 tablespoons Pernod
- Confectioners' sugar, for sprinkling
- 1 small head of fennel, sliced thin and diced
- 1 pint strawberries, tops removed and sliced

Preheat the oven to 350 degrees F. Line a half sheet pan (18 x 13 inches) with parchment paper and spray with nonstick cooking spray.

To prepare the sponge cake, beat the eggs in an electric mixer fitted with a whip attachment on medium speed. Add the sugar in thirds until incorporated. Fold in the flour with a rubber spatula, then fold in the butter. Fold in the vanilla and salt.

Bake for 12–15 minutes, until the top springs back when lightly pressed and a toothpick inserted in the center comes out clean.

Cool on a wire rack. Slice into $1/4$-inch strips that are the full length of the pan.

To prepare the filling, beat the cream cheese with an electric mixer fitted with the paddle attachment until smooth. Add the manchego cheese, milk, and butter; beat until smooth. Set aside.

In a clean bowl, beat the egg whites, cream of tartar, and $2/3$ cup sugar to form peaks that are stiff but not dry.

In separate bowl, beat the remaining sugar, egg yolks, honey, lemon juice, and cornstarch until smooth. Fold the egg yolk mixture into the cheese mixture in the electric mixer using a paddle attachment. Remove from the mixer and fold in the egg whites with a rubber spatula.

Preheat the oven to 375 degrees F. Line a 9 x 11-inch baking pan with parchment paper and butter the paper and sides of the pan. Slice the sponge cake into $1/2$-inch-thick pieces and cover the entire bottom of the pan, letting the pieces touch. Pour the manchego cheese filling over the sponge cake to fill the pan.

Bake for 30–35 minutes, until batter is set and a toothpick inserted in the middle comes out dry. Let cool and remove from pan.

To make the strawberry compote, put fennel seeds into a saucepan and toast over low heat until they smoke. Add sugar, lemon juice, and Pernod; cook over medium heat until sugar dissolves. Add the diced fennel and cook until translucent. Add strawberries and cook another 15–20 minutes. Remove from heat and cool. Serve at room temperature.

To serve, cut the cheesecake into desired serving sizes. Serve with strawberry fennel compote and sprinkle with confectioners' sugar.

Sweet Potato Pie

BUSY BEE CAFÉ, OWNER TRACY GATES

Makes 2 pies

The Southern classic, served at an Atlanta classic.

1½ cups cooked, mashed sweet potatoes

¾ cup evaporated milk

2 large eggs, beaten

1 cup sugar

¼ cup unsalted butter, melted

¼ teaspoon ground mace

½ teaspoon ground nutmeg

½ teaspoon vanilla extract

¼ teaspoon coconut extract

2 (9-inch) unbaked pie shells

Preheat the oven to 350 degrees F.

Combine the potatoes, evaporated milk, eggs, sugar, butter, mace, nutmeg, vanilla, and coconut extract. Blend until smooth. Divide the mixture between the two pie shells.

Bake for 30–45 minutes, until the centers of the pies seem set but still jiggle. Let cool on a rack, then refrigerate.

Bailey's Soufflé with Mocha Chocolate Chip Crème Fraîche

NIKOLAI'S ROOF, CHEF OLIVIER DE BRUSSCHERE

Makes 8 individual soufflés

How appropriate: Nikolai's mile-high city view reminds us of this skyscraping dessert.

Soufflé Base

- 1/2 quart whole milk
- 1 vanilla bean
- 4 egg yolks
- 3 tablespoons granulated sugar
- 2 tablespoons flour
- Pinch salt
- 1 tablespoon cornstarch
- 1/4 cup Bailey's liqueur

Soufflé

(These should be baked in individual soufflé pans but can all be baked at the same time.)

- 1/2 cup butter
- 1/2 cup sugar
- 1/2 cup heavy cream
- 1 tablespoon mocha extract
- 1 tablespoon chocolate chips
- 3 egg whites
- 1 1/2 teaspoons cornstarch

To prepare the soufflé base, combine the milk and whole vanilla bean in a small saucepan and bring to a boil. Remove from heat and remove the vanilla bean pod.

In a medium bowl, whisk together the egg yolks, sugar, flour, salt, and cornstarch until light. Very slowly stir the milk mixture into the sugar mixture. Return to the saucepan and bring to a boil while

stirring frequently. Return to the bowl and let cool. Whisk in Bailey's liqueur.

Preheat the oven to 350 degrees F. Generously butter a 1 cup soufflé dish. Sprinkle with a few tablespoons sugar and swirl to coat.

Whip the cream until firm. Fold in the mocha extract and chocolate chips.

In a large clean bowl, beat the egg whites until foamy. Fold in the cornstarch and mix together with 4 tablespoons of the soufflé base. Pour into the soufflé dish.

Bake for about 10 minutes, until well risen and beginning to brown. Serve hot, topped with the mocha whipped cream.

Coconut Cake

CARVER'S COUNTRY KITCHEN,
OWNERS ROBERT AND SHARON CARVER

Served 10 to 12

Traditionalists will love this unadulterated, old-fangled favorite.

Cake

- 1 (18.5-ounce) box yellow cake mix
- 3 large eggs
- 1/3 cup vegetable oil
- 3/4 cup pineapple juice
- 1 small very ripe banana, chopped
- 1 teaspoon coconut extract
- 1/2 (12-ounce) can evaporated milk
- 1/2 (14-ounce) can condensed milk
- 1 teaspoon vanilla extract

Frosting

- 1 (8-ounce) tub Cool Whip
- 1 teaspoon coconut extract
- 1/2 cup butter, at room temperature
- 8 ounces (or 1/2 package) confectioners' sugar
- Shredded coconut, to garnish

Preheat the oven according to package directions and prepare one 9 x 13-inch baking pan or two 8-inch round pans according to the cake mix directions.

To make the cake, combine the cake mix, eggs, oil, pineapple juice, banana, and coconut extract in a large bowl. Beat with an electric mixer on medium speed for 3 minutes. Pour into prepared pan(s).

Bake according to the package directions. While the cake bakes, combine the evaporated milk, condensed milk, and vanilla in a saucepan and heat until warm to allow the condensed milk to mix well.

When the cake is done, remove it from the oven. Poke holes all over the cake with a fork and pour the milk mixture over the cake. Let cool in the pan(s).

Invert the cake onto a cake dish if you are making a layer cake, or leave in the baking dish if you are making a sheet cake.

To prepare the frosting, combine the Cool Whip and coconut extract in the bowl of an electric mixer with the butter and confectioners' sugar. Beat until smooth. Frost the cake. Sprinkle with coconut.

Lemon Chess Pie

HORSERADISH GRILL, CHEF DANIEL ALTERMAN

Makes 2 pies

A perfect traveling companion for a late afternoon picnic.

Pie crust

Makes 2 (9- or 10-inch) shells

- 3 cups flour
- 1½ teaspoons salt
- 1½ cups sugar
- 1 cup butter, very cold and cut into cubes
- ¼ cup lard, very cold
- ¾ cup water, very cold

Whipped cream
Fresh strawberries
Fresh blackberries
Confectioners' sugar

Lemon Filling

- ⅓ cup butter, melted
- 1½ cups sugar
- 4 eggs
- 1 tablespoon flour
- 1 tablespoon cornmeal
- ¼ teaspoon salt
- ⅓ cup lemon juice
- ½ cup buttermilk
- 1 tablespoon vanilla extract

Preheat the oven to 275 degrees F.

To make the pie shell, mix together all ingredients except for the water, and pulse for 5 or 6 seconds. The mixture will have the consistency of small peas. Then add water a little at a time, and pulse until the dough forms into a ball. When the dough balls, stop adding the water.

Roll out two pie crusts and transfer to two 9- or 10-inch pie plates. Pat along the bottom and up the sides of the pan to form an even crust. Flute the edges.

Bake for 30–35 minutes, or until the crust begins to brown. Let cool.

To make the filling, whisk together the butter, sugar, eggs, flour, cornmeal, salt, lemon juice, buttermilk, and vanilla. Pour into the baked pie crusts and bake at 275 degrees F for 15–20 minutes. Refrigerate overnight.

To serve, cut the pie into six wedges. Garnish each slice with whipped cream and fresh berries. Sprinkle with confectioners' sugar and serve.

Chocolate Fried Pies

SAWICKI'S GROCERY, CHEF/OWNER LYNNE SAWICKI

Makes 6 to 8 pies

Sweet, snappy, cool, hot, crunchy, and gooey, Sawicki's version of the Georgia classic covers all the bases.

Pastry

- 2 cups flour, plus more as needed
- 1 tablespoon baking powder
- 1 tablespoon sugar
- 1 teaspoon salt
- 6 tablespoons unsalted butter, cold and cut into small pieces
- 3/4 cup milk

Chocolate Filling

- 1/2 cup heavy cream
- 10 ounces dark (58 percent cacao) chocolate, finely chopped
- Soybean, vegetable, or peanut oil for frying

To make the pastry, combine the flour, baking powder, sugar, and salt in a mixing bowl. By hand or with a mixer, cut in butter until it is about the size of small peas. Mix in the milk until the dough forms a ball. Add extra flour if the dough is too sticky.

On a lightly floured surface, roll out to a thickness of 1/4 inch. Cut into six to eight 4-inch rounds; cover and refrigerate while you prepare the filling.

Put 1 to 2 ounces of chocolate aside for plating. To make the chocolate filling, heat the heavy cream and pour it over the remaining chocolate. Mix together until the chocolate is melted and the mixture has a glossy finish. Refrigerate until fully cooled.

To assemble the pies, place the pastry rounds on a work surface. Using a 1-ounce ice cream scoop, spoon 1 ounce of filling onto the center of each pastry circle, fold over to make a semicircle, and crimp the edges to seal. You may freeze the pies at this point.

Preheat 3 inches of oil to 350 degrees F. Slide the pies into the oil and fry until golden brown, about 7 minutes.

Melt the remaining reserve chocolate in a double-boiler over medium heat and allow to cool. To serve, drizzle 1/4 teaspoon melted chocolate on top of the pie.

Chantilly Cream

SOUTH CITY KITCHEN,
OWNER DEAN DUPUIS

Serves 4

As delicate as a lace-edged valentine, chantilly cream is like the first blush of romance: cloudy, light, and impossibly sweet. It also goes well over fresh seasonal fruit.

- 2 cups heavy cream
- 1/4 cup sugar
- 1 teaspoon vanilla extract

Pour the cream into a chilled bowl and set the bowl over ice. Whisk for a few minutes until the cream starts to thicken. Slowly add the sugar and continue to whip until soft peaks form. Beat in the vanilla extract and chill until serving.

Rhubarb Preserves

SOUTH CITY KITCHEN,
OWNER DEAN DUPUIS

Makes 4 cups

Once grown wherever there was a good blast of sunlight, rhubarb's distinctive sweet-tart taste is making a comeback.

- 1 1/4 pounds frozen rhubarb
- 2 1/4 cups sugar
- 2 tablespoons freshly squeezed lemon juice

Combine the rhubarb, sugar, and lemon juice in a saucepan over medium heat and bring to a simmer. Cook until the rhubarb breaks down and mixture is syrupy but not caramelized, 15–20 minutes. Cool and store in the refrigerator.

Very Good Chocolate Cake

WATERSHED, CHEF SCOTT PEACOCK

Serves 8 to 12

A little patience in the making translates into deep appreciation for the outcome.

2 cups sugar

1½ cups cake flour

¾ teaspoon baking soda

½ teaspoon salt

1 cup hot double-strength
   brewed coffee

4 ounces unsweetened
   chocolate, finely chopped

2 large eggs, at room
   temperature

½ cup vegetable oil

½ cup sour cream, at
   room temperature

1½ teaspoons vanilla extract

Frosting

1 cup heavy whipping cream

½ cup unsalted butter, cut
   into ½-inch pieces

⅓ cup granulated sugar

¼ teaspoon salt

1 pound semisweet chocolate,
   finely chopped

¼ cup hot double-strength
   brewed coffee

1 teaspoon vanilla extract

Preheat the oven to 325 degrees F. Line two 9-inch cake pans with parchment paper and butter and flour the paper.

To make the cake, sift together the sugar, flour, baking soda, and salt in a bowl.

Pour the hot coffee over the chopped chocolate in a separate bowl and allow the chocolate to melt completely.

In a separate bowl, whisk together the eggs and vegetable oil. Whisk in the sour cream, vanilla, and coffee mixture until well blended. Stir this liquid mixture into the dry ingredients by thirds, stirring well after each addition until completely blended. Divide the batter evenly between the prepared cake pans. Drop each cake pan once onto the counter from a height of 3 inches to remove any large air pockets, which could cause holes or tunnels in the baked cake layers.

Bake for 30–40 minutes, until the cake springs back slightly when gently tapped in the center or a cake tester inserted in the center comes out clean. Remove immediately to cooling racks and allow to rest 5 minutes before turning out of the pans. Allow the cakes to cook completely before peeling off the parchment layer and spreading the frosting.

To make the frosting, heat the cream, butter, sugar, and salt in a heavy saucepan until the butter is melted. Add the chocolate and cook over a very low heat, stirring constantly, until the chocolate is melted and the mixture is smooth. Remove from the heat and blend in the coffee and vanilla.

Transfer the frosting to a bowl to cool, stirring occasionally, until it is of a spreading consistency, about 1 hour, depending on the temperature of the kitchen. If your kitchen is very warm, move the frosting to a cooler area to cool and thicken, but do not refrigerate or chill over ice water. Chocolate and butter solidify at different temperatures, and harsh chilling could cause the frosting to separate and turn grainy.

To assemble, place one cooled cake layer on a serving platter, bottom-side up, and frost the surface thickly. Top with the other layer, bottom-side down, and frost the top and sides. For best results, allow the cake to sit for 2 or more hours before slicing. Store covered at room temperature.

High-tini
Table 1280, at the High Museum

Beverages

What Would You Like to Drink . . . Besides Coke?

John Berendt's best-selling book about Savannah, *Midnight in the Garden of Good and Evil,* repeats the three telling first questions asked in Georgia's biggest cities: In Atlanta, he says, it's "What's your business?" In Macon, it's, "Where do you go to church?" In Savannah, it's, "What would you like to drink?"

We'd like to switch places with our coastal sister city for a moment, and while we retain the right to remain sober during working hours, we'd like to add a few options to your choice of beverages . . . besides, of course, the amber liquid that enriched so many of our citizens, underwrote several of our cultural institutions, and made our town famous: Coca-Cola.

Sweet Tea

THE SUNDIAL

Makes 3 quarts

Made with orange- and vanilla-bean-infused sugar syrup, the Sundial's sweet tea is perfect for watching an Atlanta sundown from the top of the Westin Peachtree Plaza.

Simple Syrup

4 cups sugar

2 cups water

8 oranges, sliced

1 vanilla bean, split lengthwise and seeds scraped

Tea

3 quarts brewed tea

Ice

To prepare the simple syrup, combine the sugar, water, oranges, and vanilla beans and bean pod, and simmer for 15 minutes. Strain the syrup and cool.

To prepare the tea, mix together the tea, ice, and sweeten to taste with the simple syrup. Left-over syrup can be refrigerated for future use. Chill before serving.

Mango Lassi

HIMALAYAS

Serves 1

This cooling yogurt-based drink is a welcome counter-point to a fiery curry or vindaloo.

  1 cup plain yogurt
  ½ cup milk
  1 cup chopped, peeled, and pitted mango
  4 teaspoons sugar
  Ground cardamom, to taste

Combine the yogurt, milk, mango, and sugar in a blender and blend for 2 minutes. Pour into a glass. Sprinkle the top with cardamom and serve, or store in the refrigerator for up to 24 hours.

Egg Cream

BAGEL PALACE

Serves 1

As every New York deli-lover knows, this sweet, foamy drink contains neither egg nor cream. Southerners might compare it to a more familiar favorite: Yoo-Hoo.

  1½ cups seltzer or soda water, divided
  ½ cup milk
  ⅓ cup chocolate syrup (Hershey's
    or your favorite brand)

Pour ¼ cup of the seltzer into a glass. Add the milk, pouring it down the side of the glass. Add the chocolate syrup, pouring it down the side of the glass. Add the remaining 1¼ cups seltzer, pouring it down the side of the glass. Stir to mix. The egg cream will foam if made properly. Serve immediately.

Uptown

BUSY BEE CAFE

Makes 2 gallon pitchers

Atlantans know there are only two kinds of iced tea: sweet and "unsweet." At the Busy Bee, you can also opt for the Uptown, combining house-brewed iced tea and homemade lemonade.

Tea

2 cups cold water

3 family-size tea bags

1 cup sugar, or to taste

Fresh Lemonade

2¼ cups sugar, or to taste

3 cups freshly squeezed lemon juice (about 20 lemons)

Warm water

To make the tea, pour water into a pot and add the tea bags. Bring to a boil and remove from the heat. Cover and let steep 10–15 minutes. Pour into a gallon pitcher and add the sugar. Stir until the sugar is dissolved.

To make the lemonade, combine the sugar and lemon juice in a gallon container. Stir in warm water until the sugar is dissolved, filling the pitcher.

To make an Uptown, fill a glass half full with tea and add lemonade until the drink is as tart as you like. Stir, add ice, and enjoy!

Afternoon Delight

SHAUN'S EDGEWOOD SOCIAL CLUB

Serves 1

Bourbon, pear cognac, and biscotti. Do you know a better way to spend an afternoon?

1½ ounces Maker's Mark bourbon
½ ounce Belle de Brillet pear cognac
½ ounce Ferretti Biscotti liqueur
Dash of angostura bitters
1 egg white
Splash of soda water
Lemon wheel

In a cocktail shaker, add all ingredients except for lemon wheel and shake. Pour over ice in a Collins glass and garnish with lemon wheel.

Bramble

SHAUN'S EDGEWOOD SOCIAL CLUB

Serves 1

If you've ever been blackberry picking as a kid, you've probably gotten caught in a bramble. This adult beverage is a much more enjoyable entrapment.

Crushed ice (see Note)

1½ ounces Bombay gin

½ ounce freshly squeezed lemon juice

½ ounce simple syrup (see Note)

½ ounce crème de cassis

Fresh blueberries or blackberries
   (or brandied cherries if berries
   are out of season), to garnish

Sliced lemon, to garnish

Fill a cocktail or martini glass with crushed ice. In a cocktail shaker with ice, combine the gin, lemon juice, and simple syrup. Shake well. Strain into the glass of crushed ice. Gently pour the crème de cassis into the glass so it travels through crushed ice to settle at bottom of glass. Garnish the drink with fresh berries and lemon and serve.

NOTES: Crush ice using a commercial ice crusher, blender, or by hand. (This can be done with a pestle and cocktail shaker or by wrapping ice in a towel and hitting against a counter top. Only soft or small ice can be crushed this way. Do not attempt with large homemade ice cubes as they will be too hard.)

To prepare simple syrup, mix equal parts white sugar and boiling water. Stir to dissolve and allow to cool.

Mint Julep

SHAUN'S EDGEWOOD SOCIAL CLUB

Serves 1

Northerners often think of the julep as Southerners' favorite, but it's often difficult to find and, when found, served far too sweet. Shaun Doty's version follows the beloved Kentucky Derby recipe, with plenty of fresh mint and crushed (not cubed) ice.

Crushed ice (see Note)

2 ounces quality bourbon (Maker's
   Mark or Knob Creek)

½ to ¾ ounce mint simple syrup (depending
   on sweetness desired) (see Note)

Fresh mint leaves, torn

Fill a tumbler or old-fashioned glass with crushed ice. (Traditionalists prefer a silver tumbler, but glass works just fine for the average person.)

Fill a cocktail shaker with ice and add the bourbon, mint syrup, and mint leaves. Shake well and strain into glass of crushed ice. Garnish with a large sprig of fresh mint.

NOTES: Crush ice using a commercial ice crusher, blender, or by hand. (This can be done with a pestle and cocktail shaker or by wrapping ice in a towel and hitting against a counter top.

Only soft or small ice can be crushed this way. Do not attempt with large homemade ice cubes as they will be too hard.)

To prepare mint simple syrup, mix 1 cup white sugar and 1 cup boiling water. Tear or crush three to four large sprigs of mint leaves and add to mixture. Allow to cool and strain out the mint before it starts to brown.

Pirate Booty

Serves 1

Beware: These chilly libations taste so good you might end up needing two eye patches.

2 lemon wheels

1½ ounces rum

½ ounce Grand Marnier

Dash of whiskey barrel bitters

Splash of ginger ale

Ice

½ ounce pomegranate syrup

Cranberry, for garnish

Muddle two lemon wheels in a rocks glass (to "muddle," you press the fruit into an empty glass to extract the juices). Remove the lemon wheels.

In a shaker, pour the rum, Grand Marnier, whiskey barrel bitters, and ginger ale; toss twice. Add ice to the glass and pour contents of shaker over the ice. Add the pomegranate syrup and a cranberry on a toothpick between two lemon wheels for garnish, and serve.

The Woodruff

Serves 1

How perfectly appropriate: named for former Coca-Cola chairman Robert Woodruff, the Woodruff Art Center restaurant's namesake drink combines his favorite liquor, bourbon, and "Georgia champagne." (Coke, for the uninitiated.)

Ice
1¼ ounces bourbon
    (Knob Creek is recommended)
Coca-Cola Classic
Lemon twist

Fill a 12-ounce rocks glass with cubed ice. Pour the bourbon over the ice. Fill with Coke. Squeeze a lemon twist over the top to release the aromatic oils.

Garnish with the lemon twist.

High-tini

Serves 1

The High Museum's companion restaurant labels this peach liqueur, cranberry juice, and agave nectar potable a "Modern mARTini."

Ice
2½ ounces vodka
    (Level brand is recommended)
1 ounce peach liqueur
    (Pallini Peachello is recommended)
Splash cranberry juice
2 wedges fresh lemon
½ ounce agave nectar, or to taste

Fill a cocktail shaker with ice. Add the vodka, peach liqueur, and cranberry juice. Squeeze the lemon wedges into shaker and leave the used wedges in the shaker.

Drizzle the agave nectar into the shaker. Shake vigorously and strain into a chilled martini glass.

Recipe Index

Boldface numbers indicate
a photograph

Index of Restaurants & Owners

Metric Conversion Chart

Volume Measurements		Weight Measurements		Temperature Conversion	
U.S.	Metric	U.S.	Metric	Fahrenheit	Celsius
1 teaspoon	5 ml	1/2 ounce	15 g	250	120
1 tablespoon	15 ml	1 ounce	30 g	300	150
1/4 cup	60 ml	3 ounces	90 g	325	160
1/3 cup	75 ml	4 ounces	115 g	350	180
1/2 cup	125 ml	8 ounces	225 g	375	190
2/3 cup	150 ml	12 ounces	350 g	400	200
3/4 cup	175 ml	1 pound	450 g	425	220
1 cup	250 ml	2 1/4 pounds	1 kg	450	230